# Introduction

Children are born with the innate desire to communicate. In the early years, they label, mimic, and experiment with language. As they develop and grow, there is a natural tendency for them to expand their love of language into written expression; first through random scribbles and symbols, and then with specific words and sentences. Yet, when many of these children come to school, they are expected to use formal writing before they are ready. When children do not yet possess the prerequisites for writing, they may become frustrated and discouraged and may have the desire to give up trying to write.

Successful writing requires four key elements:
- the desire to say something
- the vocabulary to say it
- the ability to make words
- the structure with which to say it

As young children are acquiring these prerequisites, they need support and direction. It is important to be able to determine each child's developmental level and provide activities that will serve as building blocks to help children internalize the writing process.

Rebuses are a great way to provide children with the tools they need in order to learn to write. Rebuses are a wonderful way of combining pictures and print. Children quickly learn that words are meant to convey meaning. The use of rebuses exposes children to words that are above their reading level but part of their spoken vocabulary. As young children work with rebuses, they begin to understand the reading process and how decoding and encoding work. They also develop strong print awareness and utilize their own written language to practice their emerging reading skills. With the support of rebus vocabulary, beginning writers are empowered with the tools they need to express themselves in print.

The rebuses used throughout the program presented in *Rebus Writing* are designed to teach word meaning, expand vocabulary, and provide orthographic support. The rebuses incorporate pictures and phonetic units. By having to combine the elements in the picture, children are actually sounding out the rebus and developing their decoding and encoding skills.

*Rebus Writing* features seasonal themes that integrate content learning and writing. The integrated themes include science, social studies, and seasonal concepts. Each theme introduces related vocabulary, the printed word, and a pictorial rebus to teach children about the concept and provide the words they need to write sentences and related stories. Additionally, since many of the rebus activities are based on beginning reading skills, these activities can be incorporated into reading instruction.

The rebus vocabulary and themes start out very simple. This allows children to immediately recognize a specific word and its meaning. As children become competent with the rebus format, the vocabulary and rebuses become more involved. Children experiencing rebus for the first time may respond differently than their peers. The youngest children, when asked to write, may only copy the vocabulary words from the dictionary. Other children may add the rebus pictures for the words they write.

The rebus pictures are very simple so that children can readily reproduce them. Children draw the rebus to reinforce the meaning of each word and to guarantee that they can accurately read what they wrote. As children gain confidence, they begin to combine words and write sentences.

At the beginning, emphasis is placed on adjectives so that children can develop their descriptive writing skills—a sentence with describing words or a descriptive story. As the themes progress, nouns, adjectives, and verbs are all used so that children can learn about word functions and expand beyond pattern sentences. The rebus vocabulary, in conjunction with related shared reading and "read aloud" books, gives children the background they need to formulate ideas and facilitate informational writing.

Beginning with the first theme, children cut and paste the rebus vocabulary into a picture dictionary. This provides each child with a "reference book" to use as he or she completes related activities and writes about the theme. Additionally, this vocabulary can be used for phonemic awareness and phonetic development. Use the reproducibles to help children practice the writing process. The multileveled activities will help you meet the needs of children at various writing stages. As a result, all children learn the same content but write about it at their own developmental level.

Providing the building blocks of writing has never been easier!

## Winter Rebus Writing
### Combining Pictures and Print to Support Beginning Writers

**Written by**
Jo Fitzpatrick

**Editors:** Sheri Rous and Carla Hamaguchi
**Illustrator:** Darcy Tom
**Designer:** Moonhee Pak
**Cover Designer:** Barbara Peterson
**Art Director:** Tom Cochrane
**Project Director:** Carolea Williams

# Table of Contents

# Using Rebus Writing to Differentiate

Learning to write is a developmental process that involves movement through designated writing stages. In order to develop stronger writing skills and move through these levels, children need to understand the writing process and how to express and organize ideas before putting them into print. For many, this is not an automatic or a natural process. Children need guidance and practice before they can easily turn oral language into written language.

To meet the needs of your children, complete the activities as a whole group, in small groups, or independently. They can be done orally with younger writers or collaboratively by writing on an enlarged reproducible page. Or, invite children to work with a partner to create sentences or stories. The independent or center activities include an art project and additional vocabulary. You can easily differentiate the activities to help children work at their own ability level. Use the follow-up activities for more advanced writers.

The activities in *Rebus Writing* are designed to give support to children at each and every beginning writing stage. The developmental activities for each theme use the rebus vocabulary to help children develop and expand their ideas. The activities involve individual student writing using support vocabulary; a Rebus Dictionary, pocket chart words, and related word webs are included in each theme. The level of difficulty can be adjusted to the needs and competency of the children and can range from sentence writing to story development. Beginning writers will become familiar with words and their meaning, while more advanced writers will be able to practice their spelling. Children will gain experience with different writing types: descriptive, narrative, and informational. Emphasis is placed on the following skills:

- sentence formation
- elaboration and expansion of ideas
- cloze completion
- sequence of events
- application of content

Children, no matter their ability level, will have access to the same content and information. They will be able to rely on their skill, interest, and readiness levels to apply this information. Adjust or tier the difficulty and focus of the activities (i.e., producing words, sentences, or stories) to differentiate the instruction based upon developmental needs.

The Rebus Approach provides built-in differentiation. Due to the nature of the program, children are able to use content to become self-improving writers. Young writers take and use the rebus and support activities at "face value" and learn how to use and combine words to develop meaningful sentences. Early writers use the support system to learn how to expand and elaborate ideas and develop related stories. More advanced writers use the Rebus Approach as a springboard to expand the informational content in their writing and to experiment with different writing genres. No matter the writing stage, the Rebus Approach empowers all children to become highly motivated and productive writers.

It is easy to address each child's developmental level. With exposure and practice, children will progress, at their own pace, from simple word writing to sentence and story writing. The activities included in each theme can be adapted accordingly. They can be done orally, as an interactive lesson, or independently for more advanced writers. The scope of the activities ranges from simple to more complex and can be used accordingly with children at various writing stages.

# Getting Started

Initially, the rebuses might seem a little overwhelming to you, especially when looking at them in their entirety. However, it is important to remember that children learn the rebuses as they go. As they learn them, so do you. After a while, the graphics become second nature and you will begin to think in terms of rebuses! Use the following steps to make each child's rebus writing experience more memorable.

**STEP 1**

There are certain standard graphics that form the rebus vocabulary. It is important to be aware of these graphics and what they represent. Review the **Graphics for Phonetic Elements** (page 10), the **Positional Vocabulary** (page 11), and the **Everyday Rebuses** (page 12) to help you internalize the basic graphics that appear in the rebus vocabulary. You can also refer to these lists if you make rebuses for songs, charts, and other materials.

**STEP 2**

Prepare a **Picture Dictionary** for each child by either purchasing a 40-page, 8½" x 6⅞" (21.5 cm x 18 cm) composition book for each child or placing 40 pieces of blank paper into a folded piece of construction paper and stapling the left side. Write each child's name on the cover of the book. Make a few extra dictionaries in case a new child comes to class during the year. As children work in their dictionary, add the picture cards to the additional dictionaries.

**STEP 3**

Read aloud a **content-related book** that relates to the theme of study. This will provide children with some background knowledge and give them a chance to hear some of the theme words in context. A list of suggested literature selections is included on the section opener page for each theme of study. Continue reading additional theme-related books throughout the theme to help reinforce it.

**STEP 4**

Review the **section opener** page for the theme of study. This page provides information about the theme, a list of theme-related literature selections, a list of "Have-To Words," Sequence Story Pocket Chart Words, a Sequence Story Prompt, and Descriptive Story Pocket Chart Words.

**STEP 5**

As children write about the theme, they use many high-frequency words that are not in their Picture Dictionary. It is important that children spell these words correctly. If left to invented spelling and sounding out, errors will appear, be repeated, and then learned. **Have-To Words** are words that children have to learn to read and spell. These words have been incorporated into each theme and appear throughout the activities. Create a **Have-To Board** on a bulletin board. Write the Have-To Words from the unit of study on separate sentence strips, and attach the sentence strips to the bulletin board. Number the words, and place them in rows of up to five words. Add additional words from other classroom studies, as needed. Have children read and spell the words on the board. If a child needs assistance finding a word, tell the child to look in a specific row or give the child the number of the desired word. As children master each word, remove it from the board.

**STEP 6**

The **Directed Activities** section (pages 13–21) includes numerous activities and reproducibles that teach and reinforce the rebus words for each theme. Children practice their writing in a whole-class or small-group setting while gaining confidence in their skills.

**STEP 7**

The **Independent or Writing Center Activities** section (pages 22–25) provides even the youngest writer with an opportunity to use support vocabulary to process information, formulate ideas, and then put those ideas down on paper. The degree of difficulty can be adjusted from simple sentence writing to story development. In each theme, emphasis is placed on descriptive writing, informational writing, and sequential writing. A reproducible is included for each activity. Either have children work independently or in a writing center to complete the activities.

**STEP 8**

Activities rotate through the themes. For example, each theme has a Word Hunt activity. Read the activity directions (page 14) and use the **Rebus Page Number Box** at the top of each activity to find the accompanying reproducible for the theme you have chosen. For example, the Word Hunt reproducible for the Reindeer theme is on page 29.

| THEME | | | | | | |
|---|---|---|---|---|---|---|
| **PAGE** | 29 | 46 | 63 | 81 | 98 | 115 |

# Organizational Tips

*Rebus Writing* is an extensive resource for teachers of beginning writers. Differentiation and developmental instruction is built right into the program. Everything you need is here, including support materials, instructional word cards, and numerous activities.

All types of student grouping and instructional strategies can be used with the activities in this resource, depending on the range of ability levels in your classroom and your teaching style and preference. You can elect to complete the activities in whole-group, small-group, or independent settings. The following suggestions are made to serve as a springboard to help you design the best organizational plan that meets your children's particular needs.

## WHOLE-GROUP INSTRUCTION

- Read-alouds
- Shared reading
- Have-To Words
- Introduction of rebus vocabulary
- Picture Dictionary
- Secret Sentence Booklets
- Bubble Writing
- Connect a Sentence

## SMALL-GROUP (SKILL-BASED) INSTRUCTION

Group students according to their developmental needs for these activities:
- Sentence Squares
- Sentence/Story Builder
- Story Box
- Backward Story

## SMALL-GROUP (HETEROGENEOUS) INSTRUCTION

Group students in small groups that consist of varied ability levels or as a center activity. Allow advanced students to work independently.
- Descriptive Story
- Shape Book
- Class Book
- Sequence Story

# Basic Rebuses

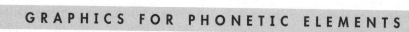
The following graphics are used in many phonetic words to help children learn and apply the decoding process. These phonetic sounds are represented with a rebus that is related to the actual sound. Use the phrase to explain the rebus.

**/th/**    the stick-out-your-tongue sound

**/sh/**    the quiet sound

**/ou/**    the hammerhead sound
(what you say when you hit your finger with a hammer)

**/oo/**    the ghost sound

**/ing/**    the king of the *ing* sound

**/ch/**    the choo choo sound

**/oo/**    the muscle man sound
(what you say when you lift something heavy)

er$^{rrr}$ **/er/**    hold onto the *r* (*ir* and *ur*)

**/u/**    the belly button sound—like when you poke yourself in the belly button
(this is used for the short *u* sound and the schwa sound)

**"A"** Note: If the rebus is in quotes, say the name of the letter (for use with long vowel sounds). Use this when a letter name is a sound (e.g., /ar/ = "R" or candy =   + "D").

The following words use the above graphics. Once you get used to the phonetic graphics, you will see how easy it is to come up with rebuses for practically any word you want.

| | | | |
|---|---|---|---|
| 😛+"A" | "E"+🚂 | r+👻+ m | 😛+👑 |
| **they** | **each** | **room** | **thing** |
| m+"A"+K | t+✊🔨+n | l+er$^{rrr}$+n | 🤫+🏋️+d |
| **make** | **town** | **learn** | **should** |

## POSITIONAL VOCABULARY

The following rebuses help describe locations. Write the rebuses on the board. As you introduce each rebus, say the phrase so children will understand the graphic.

the dot is **in** the box

the dot is **out** of the box

the dot is **on** the box

the dot is **over** the box

the dot is **under** the box

the dot fell **from** the shelf

the dot is **between** the lines

the dot is **after** the line

the dot is **before** the line

the dot is **at** the line

the dot is at the **top** of the paper

the dot is at the **bottom** of the paper

The following rebuses are used for basic vocabulary. Write the rebuses on the board. Say each phrase when you introduce the rebus to children.

it **is** a line

it is **a** belly button

that means **was**

**has**—breathe out and say /s/

one circle **with** another

the car **went** down the street

**give** me the box

I **did** it

**who**—what an owl says

**where** in the world are you

it is a dot

"R"
it's an **R** for the word are

w+er<sup>rr</sup>
this says **were**

I **have** the dot

w+
**will**—/w/ + ill in bed

d+
**do**—/d/ + the ghost sound

I **gave** him the box

+nt
**didn't**—did + /nt/

**what**'s in the box

"Y"
**why**—the letter "y"

pointing to **the** ___

it's a **saw**

one line **and** another

I **had** the dot but dropped it

I **want** the dot

the **don't** symbol

S+⊙+m
**some**—/s/ + belly button + /m/

I **made** it with my hands

**when**—day or night

**away**—belly button + one-way sign

# Picture Dictionary

| THEME | 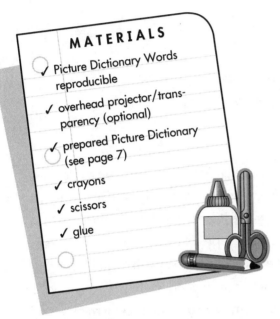 rain+d+ear | snowman | penguin+S | hamster+S | hands+S | pr+s+ss+O+car+S |
|-------|------|------|------|------|------|------|
| PAGE | 27 | 44 | 61 | 79 | 96 | 113 |

## MATERIALS

- ✓ Picture Dictionary Words reproducible
- ✓ overhead projector/transparency (optional)
- ✓ prepared Picture Dictionary (see page 7)
- ✓ crayons
- ✓ scissors
- ✓ glue

## FOCUS

Children will
- expand vocabulary.
- practice word recognition.

Copy a class set of the Picture Dictionary Words reproducible, and copy it onto an overhead transparency. Display the transparency, and discuss with children each rebus picture and what the word means. To reinforce the meaning of each word, have children practice reading it using the rebus pictures. After you have introduced all 12 words, give a clue for one of the words and have children identify it. Give each child a Picture Dictionary Words reproducible and a prepared Picture Dictionary. Have children use the appropriate color crayon to shade the color rebus. Then, have children cut out each box and glue the boxes in numerical order in their Picture Dictionary. Ask children to glue the first six pictures on the first page of their dictionary and the remaining six pictures on the second page. Then, have them label the pages with the correct theme heading. Have children keep their dictionary at their desk. To extend the activity, say a number and have children find the word in their dictionary and read it aloud.

# Word Hunt

| THEME |  +d+ 👂 | ☃ | 🐧 +S | 🐹 +S | 🤝 +S | pr+sˢˢ+◎+🚗 +s |
|---|---|---|---|---|---|---|
| PAGE | 29 | 46 | 63 | 81 | 98 | 115 |

## MATERIALS
✓ Word Hunt reproducible
✓ Picture Dictionaries (see page 13)

## FOCUS

Children will
• practice word recognition.
• use dictionary skills.

Have children point to each word for the theme of study in their Picture Dictionary as you say the word aloud. Give each child a Word Hunt reproducible. Point to the pictures on the reproducible. Explain to the class that they are to use their Picture Dictionary to locate the matching picture and write the corresponding word on the line underneath the picture on their reproducible. Tell children that at the bottom of the page they will discover a surprise sentence to complete. Point to the bracket and explain that this symbol means to start the sentence with a capital letter. Point to the dot at the end of the sentence. Explain that the dot represents a period and is at the end of a sentence. To extend the activity, write additional sentences on the board for children to complete. Note: Once children understand how to complete the activity, word practice may no longer be necessary.

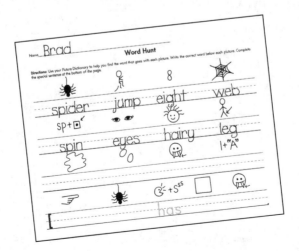

# Secret Sentence Booklet

| THEME | 🌧+d+👂 | ☃ | 🐧+S | 🦫+S | 🤝+S | pr+sˢˢ+◎+🚗+S |
|---|---|---|---|---|---|---|
| PAGE | 30–31 | 47–48 | 64–65 | 82–83 | 99–100 | 116–117 |

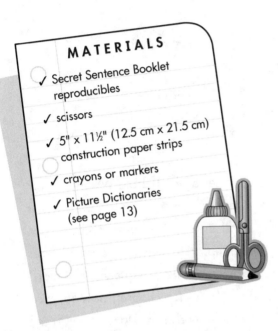

## MATERIALS

✓ Secret Sentence Booklet reproducibles

✓ scissors

✓ 5" x 11½" (12.5 cm x 21.5 cm) construction paper strips

✓ crayons or markers

✓ Picture Dictionaries (see page 13)

## FOCUS

Children will

• expand vocabulary.

• write sentences.

Copy the Secret Sentence Booklet reproducibles for each child. Cut the reproducibles in half lengthwise on the line. Assemble them in numerical order. Staple the left side of a construction paper strip to the front and back of the reproducibles to make a booklet. Give each child a prepared Secret Sentence Booklet. Draw a rebus sentence (pictures only) from the reproducible on the board. Point to each rebus picture, and have children say the word that goes with the rebus. Next, write the word under the picture. Read the word for the picture. Emphasize to children that the word is written right under the picture to allow for space between words. Continue adding each remaining word under the correct rebus picture. Have children count the rebus pictures and words on the board. Ask them to open their Secret Sentence Booklet. Point to the bracket in the booklet and remind children that this symbol means to start the sentence with a capital letter. Have children trace each bracket with a green crayon or marker. Then, point to the dot at the end of each sentence and remind children that the dot represents a period and is the end of a sentence. Have children color each period with a red crayon or marker. Invite them to read the first rebus sentence in their booklet to discover what the Secret Sentence says. Have children use their Picture Dictionary to help them write each word under the appropriate picture. Have children complete one sentence in their booklet each day until they have completed all the sentences. Encourage them to read aloud their sentences.

# Bubble Writing

| THEME | 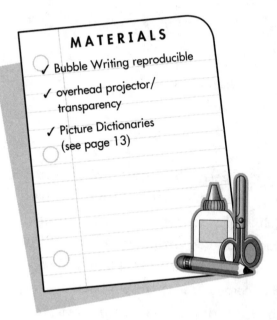+d+👂 | ☃ | 🐧+S | 🐹+S | 🤝+S | pr+s^ss+◎+🚗+s |
|---|---|---|---|---|---|---|
| PAGE | 32 | 49 | 66 | 84 | 101 | 118 |

## MATERIALS

✓ Bubble Writing reproducible

✓ overhead projector/ transparency

✓ Picture Dictionaries (see page 13)

**FOCUS**

Children will
- practice word recognition.
- write sentences.

Copy a class set of the Bubble Writing reproducible. Copy it onto an overhead transparency, and display the transparency. Give each child a reproducible. Point to the pictures in the bubbles. Invite volunteers to "read" each rebus. Model for children how to write the words for the rebuses. Have children use their Picture Dictionary to help them write the correct word from each bubble. Explain to children that each blank in the sentence has a number that corresponds with the numbered bubbles. Show children how to use the numbered words in the bubbles to complete the numbered cloze sentences on the bottom of the page. Invite volunteers to read aloud the completed sentences.

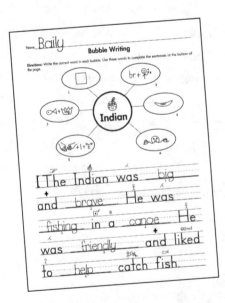

# Connect a Sentence

| THEME | +d+👂 | ⛄ | 🐧+S | 🐹+S | 🤝+S | pr+sˢˢ+◎+🚗+S |
|-------|------|------|------|------|------|------|
| PAGE | 33 | 50 | 67 | 85 | 102 | 119 |

## MATERIALS

✓ Connect a Sentence reproducible

✓ overhead projector/ transparency

✓ writing paper

✓ crayons (optional)

## FOCUS

Children will

- write pattern sentences.
- expand rebus vocabulary.
- combine ideas.

Copy a class set of the Connect a Sentence reproducible. Copy it onto an overhead transparency, and display the transparency. Discuss the rebus pictures and their word meaning with the class. Give each child a reproducible. Have children combine the phrase in the center bubble with words from the connecting bubbles to create sentences and write them on a piece of paper. Explain to children that they need to choose words that make sense in a sentence. Ask if it makes sense to say *The bear looks funny and cute.* (yes) Ask if it makes sense to say *The bear looks big and little.* (no) Encourage children to combine words from more than one bubble to expand their sentences. To extend the activity, choose a word that appears in a bubble and have children trace the bubble with a given color crayon. Repeat this process with seven additional bubbles and crayons. Say a color or invite a volunteer to say a color, and have children read the center bubble and then add the word that appears in the corresponding color bubble. For example, if you say the color red, children read the center bubble and then finish the sentence with the text that appears in the red bubble (e.g., *The bear looks hungry*).

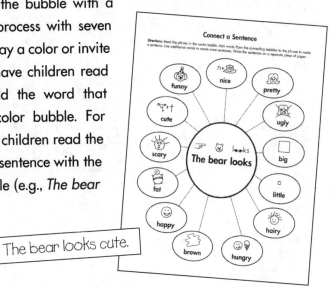

The bear looks cute.

# Sentence Squares

| THEME |  | | | | | |
|---|---|---|---|---|---|---|
| | ☁+d+👂 | ⛄ | 🐧+S | 🐹+S | 🤝+S | pr+s+🚗+s |
| **PAGE** | 34 | 51 | 68 | 86 | 103 | 120 |

## MATERIALS

✓ Sentence Squares reproducible

✓ construction paper or card stock

✓ scissors

## FOCUS

Children will practice sentence formation.

Copy a class set of the Sentence Squares reproducible onto construction paper or card stock for durability. Give each child a reproducible. Have children cut apart their squares. Say a short sentence that includes words from the reproducible. (Sample sentences are listed on the section opener page for the theme of study.) Have children select the appropriate word squares and arrange them in the correct order to make the sentence. Begin by saying the whole sentence, and then repeat the sentence a few words at a time as children find the squares to make that part of the sentence. Remind children that each sentence begins with a capital letter and ends with a punctuation mark. Repeat the process with additional sentences. To extend the activity, have children use their squares to make up their own sentences. As an option, send home the activity as homework, and have children bring back a list of the sentences they made.

Look at the funny bear

# Sentence/Story Builder

| THEME | 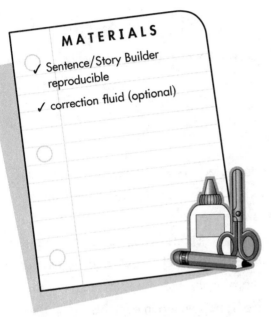 +d+ 👂 | ⛄ | 🐧+S | 🐹+S | 🤝+S | pr+sˢ+🚗+s |
|---|---|---|---|---|---|---|
| PAGE | 35 | 52 | 69 | 87 | 104 | 121 |

## MATERIALS

- ✓ Sentence/Story Builder reproducible
- ✓ correction fluid (optional)

### FOCUS

Children will develop a structured sentence or story.

Give each child a Sentence/Story Builder reproducible. Discuss the illustrations that describe *who*, *what*, *when*, *where*, and *why*. Help children use the illustrations to develop a sentence or story that includes these elements. Ask questions to help guide the sequence of the story and provide transition. For younger writers, concentrate on the composing process so children see how to connect ideas. For more advanced writers, help children formulate their ideas and model the writing process. When children are ready, have them complete the activity independently. To extend the activity, use correction fluid to delete the pictures and text from the "Is Doing What" and "Why" boxes. Have children add their own words and illustrations to these boxes and then write a story. Remind children that all sentences begin with a capital letter and end with a punctuation mark.

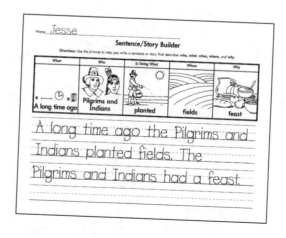

# Story Box

| THEME | ☁️+d+👂 | ⛄ | 🐧+s | 🐹+s | 🤝+s | pr+sˢˢ+◎+🚗+s |
|-------|---------|------|------|------|------|-------------|
| PAGE | 36 | 53 | 70 | 88 | 105 | 122 |

## MATERIALS

✓ Story Box reproducible

✓ overhead transparency/ projector

✓ crayons (optional)

**FOCUS**

Children will develop a story sequence.

Copy the Story Box reproducible onto an overhead transparency, and display it. Discuss with the class the character(s) and the setting. Ask questions to help children expand their thinking. Direct children's attention to the illustrations in the numbered boxes, and discuss what is happening in each box. Help children use these three pictures to combine their ideas into a sequential story. Present the activity orally with emerging writers and as a guided writing lesson with more advanced writers. Ask children questions about the illustrations to help guide the sequence of events and provide transition. As children become more comfortable with these procedures, have them complete the activity independently. Provide a list of transition words (e.g., *once, first, then, next, finally, because*) to help them connect their ideas. To extend the activity, have more capable writers illustrate their own Story Box reproducible and write a story based upon the illustrations and picture sequence.

# Backward Story

| THEME | ☁+d+👂 | ☃ | 🐧+S | 🐻+S | 🤝+S | pr+s+●+🚗+s |
|---|---|---|---|---|---|---|
| PAGE | 37 | 54 | 71 | 89 | 106 | 123 |

**MATERIALS**

✓ Backward Story reproducible

**F O C U S**

Children will understand story components and sequence.

Introduce the activity by reading aloud the end of the story as it appears on the Backward Story reproducible. Ask questions related to the story's ending to help children develop ideas for a beginning and middle. (Sample questions can be found on the reproducible.) Use the information gathered from the class discussion to help children orally organize a theme-related story with a beginning, middle, and ending. Have more advanced writers write their own story following a group discussion to gather and expand ideas. To extend the activity, have children come up with alternative story endings related to the theme. Divide the class into pairs, and have each pair of children complete a story based on the new ending.

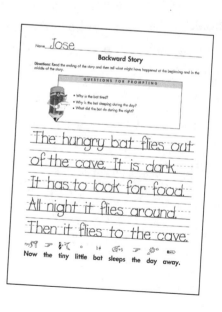

# Descriptive Story

| THEME | ☁+d+👂 | ⛄ | 🐧+S | 🐹+S | 👐+S | pr+s+◎+🚗+s |
|---|---|---|---|---|---|---|
| **PAGE** | 38 | 55 | 72 | 90 | 107 | 124 |

## MATERIALS

✓ Let's Create It reproducible

✓ Descriptive Story Pocket Chart Words reproducible

✓ card stock and laminate (optional)

✓ scissors

✓ pocket chart

✓ art materials (see Let's Create It reproducible for list of needed materials)

✓ Picture Dictionaries (see page 13)

### FOCUS

Children will use descriptive writing to write a sentence or story.

---

Make a copy of the Descriptive Story Pocket Chart Words from the page for the theme of study. As an option, copy the cards onto card stock and laminate them. Cut apart the word cards, and place them in a pocket chart. Copy a class set of the Let's Create It reproducible. Create a completed art sample following the directions on the reproducible. Review the vocabulary in the Picture Dictionary for the theme, and introduce the word cards in the pocket chart. Show children the completed sample, and review the steps they will need to follow to complete the project. Tell children that once they complete their project they are to write a sentence or story that goes with the project. Ask them to use the words from their Picture Dictionary and the word cards in the pocket chart to help them complete their writing. Have children work in a learning center to complete their project. When children have finished their project and writing, have them read their sentence or story to a partner or the whole class.

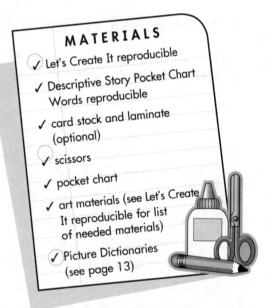

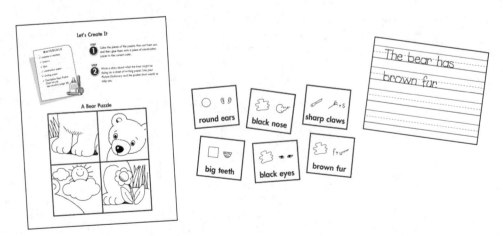

# Shape Book

| THEME | ☁️+d+👂 | ⛄ | 🐧+S | 🐹+S | 🤝+S | pr+S+⚙️+🚗+S |
|---|---|---|---|---|---|---|
| **PAGE** | 39 | 56 | 74 | 91 | 108 | 125 |

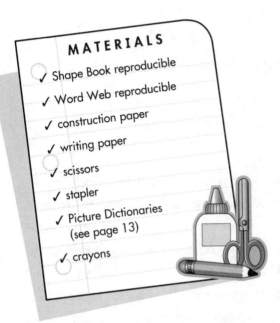

## MATERIALS

- ✓ Shape Book reproducible
- ✓ Word Web reproducible
- ✓ construction paper
- ✓ writing paper
- ✓ scissors
- ✓ stapler
- ✓ Picture Dictionaries (see page 13)
- ✓ crayons

### FOCUS

Children will practice informational writing.

Copy one class set of the Shape Book reproducible on construction paper. Copy one class set of the Word Web reproducible. As an option, laminate the Word Web reproducible for durability and place it in a learning center. Create a sample Shape Book to share with the class. Staple writing paper between a Shape Book reproducible and a blank piece of construction paper to create a booklet for each child. Demonstrate for children how to cut out the shape cover and by doing so create shaped writing paper and a back cover at the same time.

Have children review the vocabulary words in their Picture Dictionary for the appropriate theme. Tell children that they are to write about something they have learned from their theme of study. Review the words that appear on the Word Web reproducible. Invite children to share ideas about what they will write about in their shape book. Encourage them to use descriptive words in their story. Have children use their Picture Dictionary and the Word Web reproducible to help them spell the words they need to write sentences or stories in their shape book.

Invite children to color the cover of their book once their story is completed. Place the reproducibles at a learning center, and have small groups of children complete their books in the center with an adult. Younger writers may just write simple pattern sentences, while more advanced writers will combine ideas and thoughts into simple stories. Invite children to read their sentences or story to a partner or to the class.

# Class Book

| THEME | +d+👂 | ⛄ | 🐧+S | 🐹+S | 🤝+S | pr+Sˢˢ+⊙+🚗+s |
|---|---|---|---|---|---|---|
| PAGE | 41 | 58 | 76 | 93 | 110 | 127 |

## MATERIALS

✓ Class Book reproducible

✓ construction paper

✓ Picture Dictionaries (see page 13)

✓ crayons or markers

✓ bookbinding materials

## FOCUS

Children will use adjectives in a series.

Copy a class set of the Class Book reproducible. Use construction paper to make a front and back cover for the class book. Show children the cover and the reproducible. Explain to children that they will each complete a page for the class book. Tell them that the completed book will be on display so everyone will have a chance to see their "work in print" and read what their classmates wrote. Discuss the cloze activity on the reproducible, and emphasize that children will complete the sentences by using words from their Picture Dictionary and words that appear around the room. Have children complete the cloze activity at a learning center or independently. Encourage them to use their Picture Dictionary for ideas. Have an adult do the actual writing for younger children. Tell these children to read back the sentence after an adult writes it. Have children illustrate their sentence. Assemble the completed pages, add the cover to the book, and then read the book to the class. Display the book in a prominent place, and invite children to read it during free time.

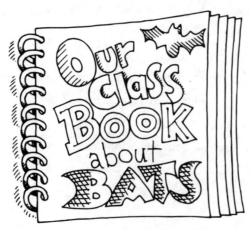

# Sequence Story

| THEME | 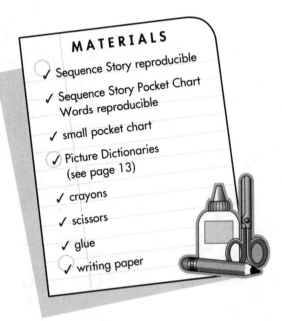 +d+👂 | ⛄ | 🐧+S | 🦫+S | 🤝+S | pr+s+🚗+s |
|---|---|---|---|---|---|---|
| PAGE | 42 | 59 | 77 | 94 | 111 | 128 |

## MATERIALS

- ✓ Sequence Story reproducible
- ✓ Sequence Story Pocket Chart Words reproducible
- ✓ small pocket chart
- ✓ Picture Dictionaries (see page 13)
- ✓ crayons
- ✓ scissors
- ✓ glue
- ✓ writing paper

### FOCUS

Children will write about a sequence of events over time.

Copy a class set of the Sequence Story reproducible. Create a sample Sequence Story to share when introducing the lesson. Make a copy of the Sequence Story Pocket Chart Words reproducible. Cut apart the word cards, and place them in a small pocket chart. Share these words with the class. Have them also review the words in their Picture Dictionary for the appropriate theme. Discuss with children the Sequence Story Prompt, which is listed on the section opener page. Show the class your Sequence Story sample. Explain to them that they will receive a series of pictures to color, cut out, and glue in proper sequence. Use the pictures from your sample as you discuss the sequence. Give each child a Sequence Story reproducible. Tell children to color, cut out, and glue the pictures in order on their reproducible. Then, have children use the Sequence Story Prompt to help them write a story about the theme on a piece of writing paper. Encourage children to use their Picture Dictionary and the pocket chart words to help them spell the words they need in order to write their sequence story. Invite volunteers to share their completed story.

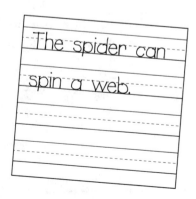

# Reindeer

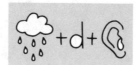

The activities in this theme emphasize the use of descriptive writing.

Additional vocabulary is introduced to promote more detailed physical descriptions and to expand children's writing to include purpose (e.g., how deer use their physical characteristics to survive).

## READ-ALOUDS

***How the Reindeer Got Their Antlers***
by Geraldine McCaughrean
(HOLIDAY HOUSE)

***Olive, the Orphan Reindeer***
by Michael Christie
(NEW CANAAN PUBLISHING COMPANY INC.)

***Olive, the Other Reindeer***
by Vivian Walsh
(CHRONICLE BOOKS)

***Rudolph Shines Again***
by Robert L. May
(GROSSET & DUNLAP)

***The Wild Christmas Reindeer***
by Jan Brett
(PUFFIN)

## PICTURE DICTIONARY WORDS

**reindeer**
**antlers**
**lose**
**sharp**
**thick**
**soft**
**fur**
**nose**
**leap**
**swimmer**
**fight**
**protect**

## POCKET CHART WORDS

| Descriptive Story | Sequence Story |
|---|---|
| furry | buck |
| white spots | doe |
| pointed ears | fawn |
| round eyes | enemies |
| soft fur | grow back |
| strong antlers | graze |

## EMPHASIZE THESE HAVE-TO WORDS IN THIS THEME:

**will**
(/w/ + ill in bed)

**them**
(stick out your tongue sound + "m")

**their**
(stick out your tongue sound + air)

**run**

**want**
(I want the dot)

## SENTENCE SQUARES SENTENCES

Reindeer are strong and fast.
They have antlers and white spots.
Reindeer like to leap and swim.
They have strong legs.
Reindeer have to protect themselves.
Reindeer have thick soft fur.

## SEQUENCE STORY PROMPT

Write a story about how the reindeer loses its antlers and grows new ones.

# Picture Dictionary Words

**Directions:** Read each word. Cut out the picture cards and glue them in your Picture Dictionary.

| | | |
|---|---|---|
| 1. <br><br> ☁️ + d + 👂 <br><br> **reindeer** | 2. <br><br> 🌿🌿 <br><br> **antlers** | 3. <br><br> l + 👻 + Z^zz <br><br> **lose** |
| 4. <br><br> 🔪 <br><br> **sharp** | 5. <br><br> 😛 + K <br><br> **thick** | 6. <br><br> ✋🛏️ <br><br> **soft** |
| 7. <br><br> f + u^rrrr <br><br> **fur** | 8. <br><br> 🙂← <br><br> **nose** | 9. <br><br> l + "E" + P <br><br> **leap** |
| 10. <br><br> 🏊 + er^rr <br><br> **swimmer** | 11. <br><br> f + 👁 + t <br><br> **fight** | 12. <br><br> 🙊 <br><br> **protect** |

# Pocket Chart Words

**Descriptive Story** (Use with Let's Create It on page 38)

| | | |
|---|---|---|
| f + u$^{rrrr}$ + "E"<br><br>**furry** | ◯  👀<br><br>**round eyes** | 🌫️  ⬛<br><br>**white spots** |
| ✋ f + u$^{rrrr}$<br><br>**soft fur** | 👆 +ed  👂 👂<br><br>**pointed ears** | 🧍 🌿 🌿<br><br>**strong antlers** |

**Sequence Story** (Use with Sequence Story on page 42)

| | | |
|---|---|---|
| b + ⊛ + k<br><br>**buck** | "N" + ⊛ + 🧍 + s<br><br>**enemies** | d + "O"<br><br>**doe** |
| 🧍 🧍<br><br>**grow back** | f + ⬜<br><br>**fawn** | gr + "A" + Z$^{zz}$<br><br>**graze** |

Rebus Writing • Winter © 2004 Creative Teaching Press

# Word Hunt

**Directions:** Use your Picture Dictionary to help you find the word that goes with each picture. Write the correct word below each picture. Complete the special sentence at the bottom of the page.

 f + u r r r r

 l + °°E'' + P

 + d + 👂 (ear)

 f + 👁 + t

 😊 + K

 + e r r r

 knife

 l + 👻 + Z zz + oo

 + d + 👂 (ear)

 hand

knife

# Secret Sentence Booklet

**Directions:** Write the correct word under each rebus picture.

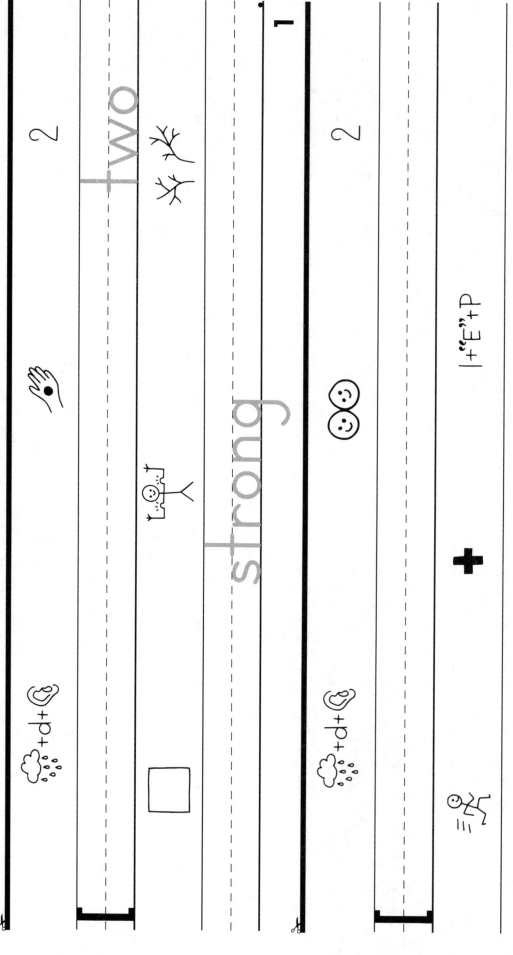

two

strong

1

run

2

# Secret Sentence Booklet

 +"A"   "U"+S$^{ss}$   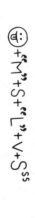 +"M"   **2**

f+🐟++   **+**

use them  themselves

🙂+"M"+S+"L"+V+S$^{ss}$

**3**

+"A"      〰〰〰   **+**

water

🐟+err+S

"R"   🙂

good

**4**

# Bubble Writing

**Directions:** Write the correct word in each bubble. Use these words to complete the sentences at the bottom of the page.

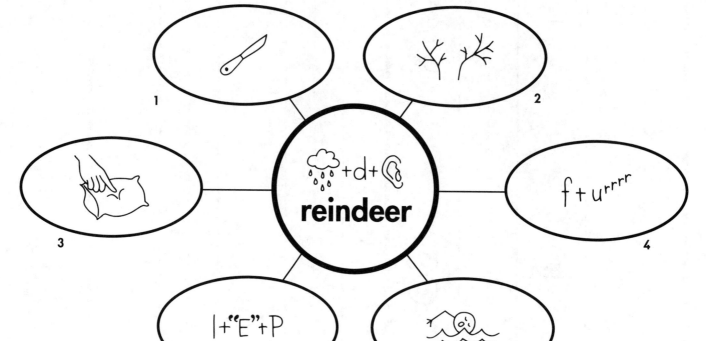

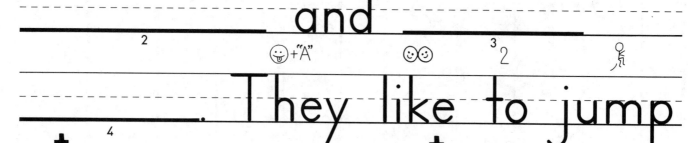

I Reindeer have _____
                              1

_____ and _____
        2                        3  2

_____. They like to jump

and _____ and _____

_____ in water.
        6

Rebus Writing • Winter © 2004 Creative Teaching Press

# Connect a Sentence

**Directions:** Read the phrase in the center bubble. Add words from the connecting bubbles to the phrase to make a sentence. Use additional words to create more sentences. Write the sentences on a separate piece of paper.

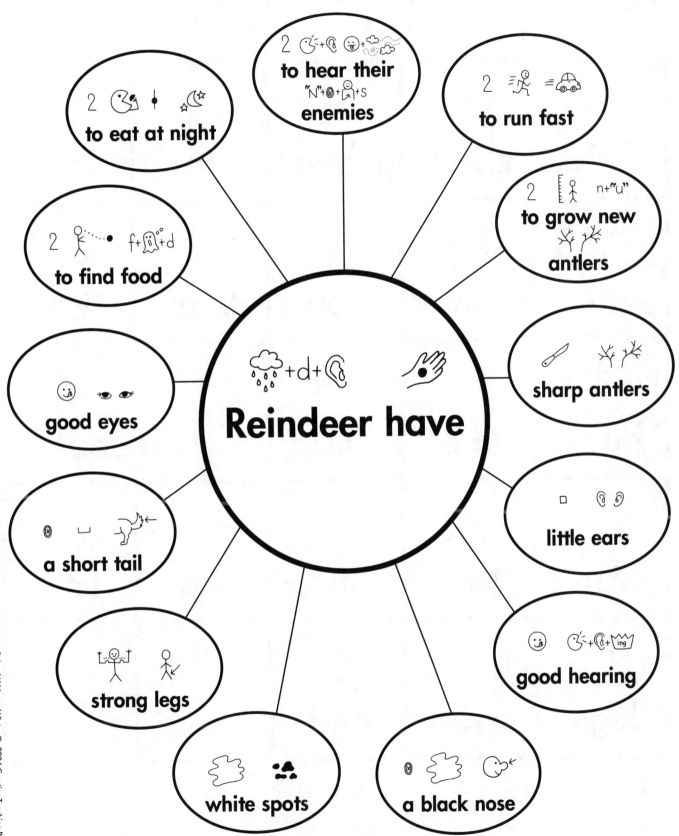

# Sentence Squares

**Directions:** Read the word cards. Cut apart the cards and mix them up. Make sure that the words are face up. Use the word cards to make sentences.

| | | | |
|---|---|---|---|
| **Reindeer** | **protect** | **to** | **run** |
| **are** | **antlers** | **strong** | **leap** | **They** |
| **have** | **like** | **thick** | **white** **spots** |
| **fur** | **fast** | **themselves** | **soft** |
| **legs** | **swim** | **and** | **.** |

Rebus Writing • Winter © 2004 Creative Teaching Press

# Sentence/Story Builder

**Directions:** Use the pictures to help you write a sentence or story that describes **who**, **what**, **when**, **where**, and **why**.

| When | Who | Is Doing What | Where | Why |
|------|-----|---------------|-------|-----|
| night | deer | hunt | forest | safe |

Name_____

# Story Box

**Directions:** Use the picture box ideas to write a story.

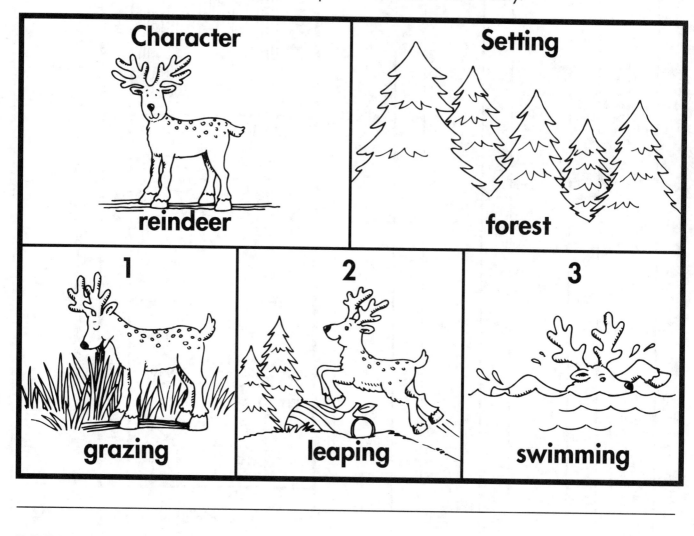

Character
reindeer

Setting
forest

1
grazing

2
leaping

3
swimming

_____
- - - - - - - - - - - - - - - - - - - -
_____
_____
- - - - - - - - - - - - - - - - - - - -
_____
_____
- - - - - - - - - - - - - - - - - - - -
_____
_____
- - - - - - - - - - - - - - - - - - - -
_____

# Backward Story

**Directions:** Read the ending of the story and then tell what might have happened at the beginning and in the middle of the story.

```
QUESTIONS FOR PROMPTING
```

- What do deer do at night?
- Where do they go?
- Why do deer eat at night?
- Who are their enemies?

_____

- - - - - - - - - - - - - - - - - - - - - - - - -

_____

- - - - - - - - - - - - - - - - - - - - - - - - -

_____

- - - - - - - - - - - - - - - - - - - - - - - - -

_____

- - - - - - - - - - - - - - - - - - - - - - - - -

_____

- - - - - - - - - - - - - - - - - - - - - - - - -

**When  daylight  comes,  the  deer  go  to  sleep.**

Rebus Writing • Winter © 2004 Creative Teaching Press

# Let's Create It

## MATERIALS

- ✓ white chalk
- ✓ 8" x 12" (20.5 cm x 30.5 cm) black construction paper
- ✓ 4" x 8" (10 cm x 20.5 cm) brown construction paper
- ✓ 4" x 8" (10 cm x 20.5 cm) writing paper
- ✓ scissors
- ✓ glue
- ✓ crayons or markers
- ✓ Descriptive Story Pocket Chart Words reproducible (page 28)

**STEP 1**

Use white chalk to trace both of your hands on black construction paper. Cut out the hands and set them aside. Trace your foot on brown construction paper and cut it out. Trace the foot pattern onto a piece of writing paper and cut it out. Glue the writing paper foot to the back of your foot cutout. Turn over the foot cutout. Glue the hand patterns to the top of the foot cutout to make antlers. Add facial features to the foot cutout to make a deer.

**STEP 2**

Use your Picture Dictionary and the pocket chart words to help you write a descriptive sentence or story about a reindeer. Read your writing to a partner.

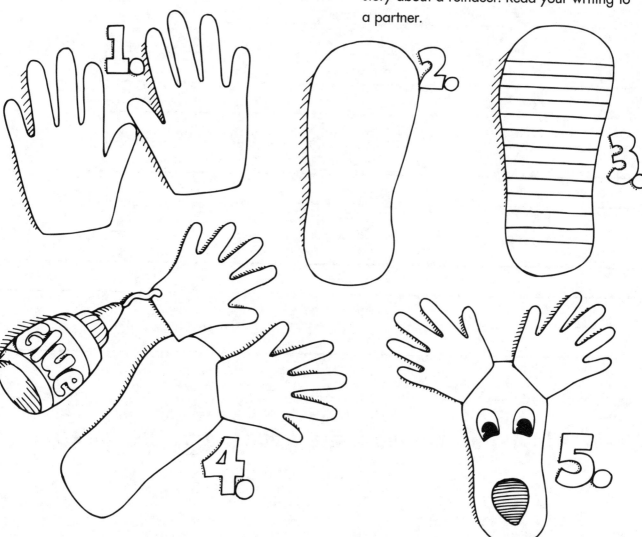

Rebus Writing • Winter © 2004 Creative Teaching Press

# Shape Book

**Directions:** Color your cover. Cut out the cover and writing paper to create a shape book.

Rebus Writing • Winter © 2004 Creative Teaching Press

# Word Web

**Directions:** Use the words on the word web to help you write a story.

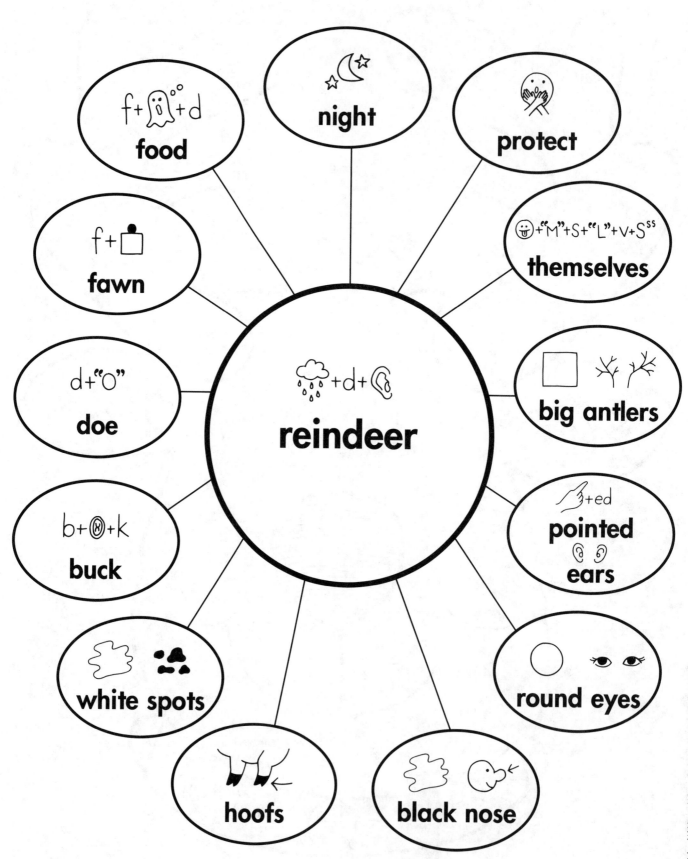

Rebus Writing • Winter © 2004 Creative Teaching Press

# Class Book

**Directions:** Use words from your Picture Dictionary and around the room to help you complete the sentences. Draw a picture to go with your sentences.

One day, I saw a _____

reindeer in the _____.

The reindeer looked _____,

_____, and _____.

The reindeer had _____.

It liked to _____

_____.

By _____

Rebus Writing • Winter © 2004 Creative Teaching Press

# Sequence Story

**Directions:** Color the pictures and cut them out. Glue the picture cards in order in the numbered boxes to show the sequence of the reindeer throughout the seasons. Use the picture cards to write a story on another piece of paper. Use your Picture Dictionary and the Sequence Story Pocket Chart Words to help you.

| | |
|---|---|
| **1** spring | **2** summer |
| **3** fall | **4** winter |

Rebus Writing • Winter © 2004 Creative Teaching Press

# Snowman

Use this theme to teach sequence. The activities in this theme emphasize the use of describing words and sequence of events. Additional vocabulary is introduced to promote descriptive writing and seasonal writing related to winter.

## READ-ALOUDS

***All You Need for a Snowman***
by Alice Schertle
(SILVER WHISTLE)

***The Biggest, Best Snowman***
by Margery Cuyler
(SCHOLASTIC)

***Snowballs***
by Lois Ehlert
(HARCOURT)

***The Snowman***
by Raymond Briggs
(RANDOM HOUSE)

***Snowmen at Night***
by Caralyn Buehner
(PHYLLIS FOGELMAN BOOKS)

## PICTURE DICTIONARY WORDS

**snowman**
**snowball**
**body**
**black hat**
**face**
**carrot nose**
**broom**
**corncob pipe**
**buttons**
**scarf**
**magic**
**funny**

## POCKET CHART WORDS

| Descriptive Story | Sequence Story |
|---|---|
| coal eyes | roll |
| berries | put together |
| sticks | cold |
| arms | sun |
| mittens | warm |
| ear muffs | melt |

## EMPHASIZE THESE HAVE-TO WORDS IN THIS THEME:

| 1st | n+"x"+t | 😊+"N" |  | |
|---|---|---|---|---|
| **first** | **next** | **then** | **made** (I made it with my hands) | **gave** (I gave him the box) |

## SENTENCE SQUARES SENTENCES

My snowman looks funny.
It is happy and magic.
I gave my snowman a carrot nose.
The snowman has a happy smile.
It has black eyes and funny buttons.
I gave my snowman a big broom.
My snowman is magic.

## SEQUENCE STORY PROMPT

Write a story that tells how to make a snowman and how it looks when it is finished.

# Picture Dictionary Words

**Directions:** Read each word. Cut out the picture cards and glue them in your Picture Dictionary.

| 1. | 2. | 3. |
|---|---|---|
| **snowman** | **snowball** | **body** |
| 4. | 5. | 6. |
| **black hat** | **face** | **carrot nose** |
| 7. | 8. | 9. |
| **broom** | **corncob pipe** | **buttons** |
| 10. | 11. | 12. |
| **scarf** | **magic** | **funny** |

Rebus Writing • Winter © 2004 Creative Teaching Press

# Pocket Chart Words

**Descriptive Story** (Use with Let's Create It on page 55)

| | | |
|---|---|---|
| K+"O"+l  👁👁 <br><br> **coal eyes** | 🐻+"E"+S <br><br> **berries** | 🌿+S <br><br> **sticks** |
| 🧍+S <br><br> **arms** | 🧤🧤 <br><br> **mittens** | 🎧 <br><br> **ear muffs** |

**Sequence Story** (Use with Sequence Story on page 59)

| | | |
|---|---|---|
| ℓℓℓ <br><br> **roll** | ✋ 2+g+😛+er^rrr <br><br> **put together** | K+👴 <br><br> **cold** |
| ☀ <br><br> **sun** | w+🧍 <br><br> **warm** | m+"L"+t <br><br> **melt** |

Name _____

# Word Hunt

**Directions:** Use your Picture Dictionary to help you find the word that goes with each picture. Write the correct word below each picture. Complete the special sentence at the bottom of the page.

   b + "D"

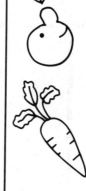  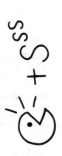

I ___ has

Rebus Writing • Winter © 2004 Creative Teaching Press

# Secret Sentence Booklet

**Directions:** Write the correct word under each rebus picture.

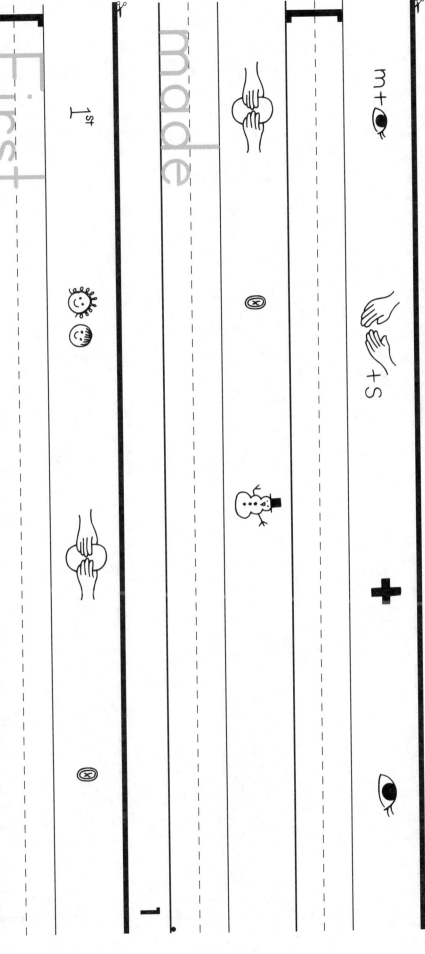

m + 👁     +     👁

✋ +S     ☃

made

🤝     Ⓧ     Ⓧ

1st

☺☺     🤝     Ⓧ

First

b + "D"     ∞     3     ❄ + O +S

with three

**1**

**2**

Rebus Writing • Winter © 2004 Creative Teaching Press

# Secret Sentence Booklet

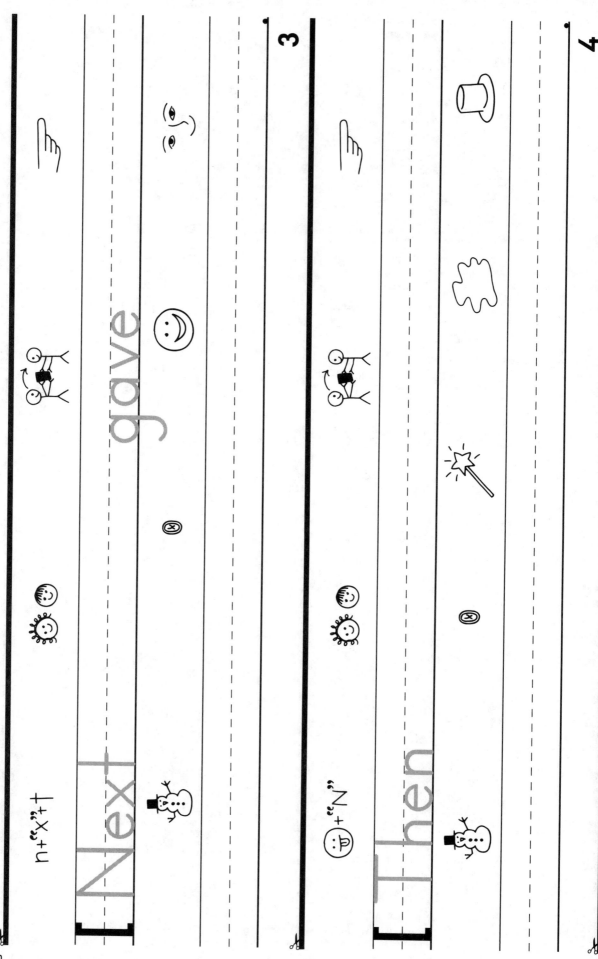

n + "x" + t   ☞   Next 🐍 ⛄

gave   ⊗   ☺ 👁👁

3

:) + "N"   ☞   Then 🐍 ⛄

⊗   🪄 🦷 🎩

4

Rebus Writing • Winter © 2004 Creative Teaching Press

# Bubble Writing

**Directions:** Write the correct word in each bubble. Use these words to complete the sentences at the bottom of the page.

# Connect a Sentence

**Directions:** Read the phrase in the center bubble. Add words from the connecting bubbles to the phrase to make a sentence. Use additional words to create more sentences. Write the sentences on a separate piece of paper.

a big smile

a candy cane

three snowballs

mittens

a corncob pipe

buttons

The snowman has

black boots

a broom

a carrot nose

a red scarf

a magic hat

coal eyes

pinecone ears

Rebus Writing • Winter © 2004 Creative Teaching Press

# Sentence Squares

**Directions:** Read the word cards. Cut apart the cards and mix them up. Make sure that the words are face up. Use the word cards to make sentences.

| | | | | |
|---|---|---|---|---|
| my | funny | I | smile | gave |
| snowman | looks | The | and | |
| magic | has | black | eyes | a |
| happy | is | carrot | nose | It |
| buttons | big | broom | . | |

# Sentence/Story Builder

**Directions:** Use the pictures to help you write a sentence or story that describes **who**, **what**, **when**, **where**, and **why**.

| When | Who | Is Doing What | Where | Why |
|------|-----|---------------|-------|-----|
| today | friends | making a snowman | backyard | play |

Rebus Writing • Winter © 2004 Creative Teaching Press

Name

# Story Box

**Directions:** Use the picture box ideas to write a story.

Characters

friends

Setting

outside

1 rolled

2 decorated

3 melted

Rebus Writing • Winter © 2004 Creative Teaching Press

# Backward Story

**Directions:** Read the ending of the story and then tell what might have happened at the beginning and in the middle of the story.

### QUESTIONS FOR PROMPTING

- Who did the magic hat belong to?
- Where did he get it?
- What happened when he put the magic hat on?

**Then     the     magic     hat     blew     away.**

Rebus Writing • Winter © 2004 Creative Teaching Press

# Let's Create It

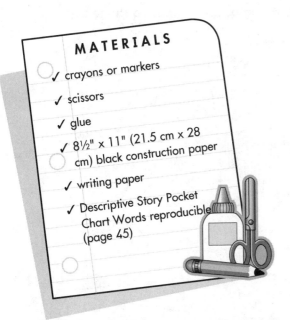

**MATERIALS**

- ✓ crayons or markers
- ✓ scissors
- ✓ glue
- ✓ 8½" x 11" (21.5 cm x 28 cm) black construction paper
- ✓ writing paper
- ✓ Descriptive Story Pocket Chart Words reproducible (page 45)

**STEP**

**1** Color the puzzle. Cut out the pieces and glue them in the correct order to a piece of black construction paper.

**STEP**

**2** Use your Picture Dictionary and the pocket chart words to help you write a story about your snowman on a separate piece of paper.

## Snowman Puzzle

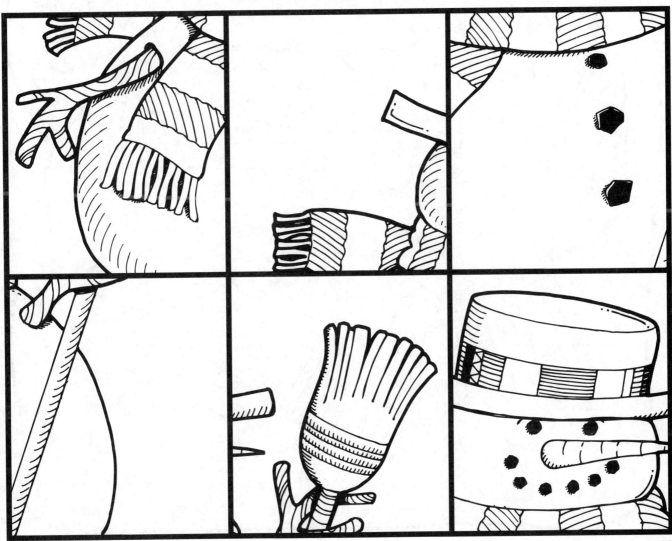

# Shape Book

**Directions:** Color your cover. Cut out the cover and writing paper to create a shape book.

Rebus Writing • Winter © 2004 Creative Teaching Press

# Word Web

**Directions:** Use the words on the word web to help you write a story.

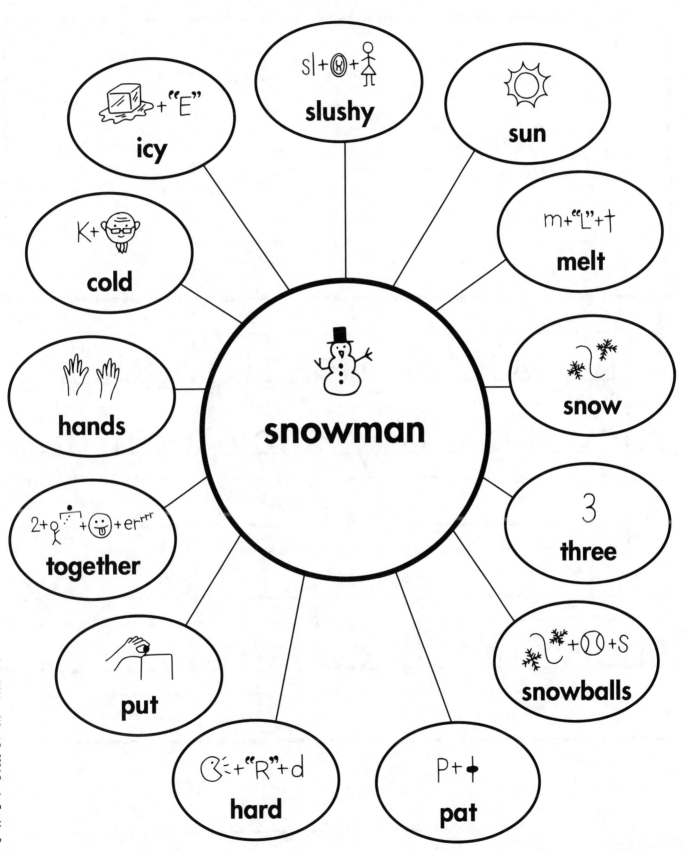

icy

slushy

sun

cold

melt

hands

snow

together

snowman

three

put

snowballs

hard

pat

Rebus Writing • Winter © 2004 Creative Teaching Press

# Class Book

**Directions:** Use words from your Picture Dictionary and around the room to help you complete the sentences. Draw a picture to go with your sentences.

1 One winter day I made a
snowman. My snowman had

a _____, a _____
and _____. I liked my

snowman because _____
_____
_____

By _____

Rebus Writing • Winter © 2004 Creative Teaching Press

# Sequence Story

**Directions:** Color the pictures and cut them out. Glue the picture cards in order in the numbered boxes to show the sequence for building a snowman. Use the picture cards to write a story on another piece of paper. Use your Picture Dictionary and the Sequence Story Pocket Chart Words to help you.

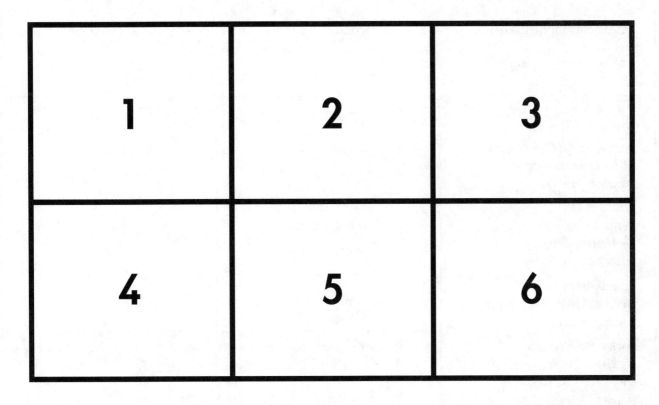

# Penguins

The activities in this theme emphasize the use of describing words and sequence of events. Additional vocabulary is introduced to promote descriptive writing and seasonal writing related to winter.

## READ-ALOUDS

***Antarctic Antics: A Book of Penguin Poems***
by Jose Aruego
(GULLIVER BOOKS)

***Penguin Pete***
by Marcus Pfister
(NORTH-SOUTH BOOKS)

***Penguins!***
by Gail Gibbons
(HOLIDAY HOUSE)

***Tacky the Penguin***
by Helen Lester
(HOUGHTON MIFFLIN)

***A Wish for Wings That Work***
by Berekely Breathed
(LITTLE, BROWN AND COMPANY)

## PICTURE DICTIONARY WORDS

**penguin**
**black and white**
**flippers**
**web feet**
**feathers**
**ice**
**water**
**play**
**swim**
**slide**
**fish**
**rookery**

## POCKET CHART WORDS

| Descriptive Story | Sequence Story |
| --- | --- |
| feathery | Daddy Penguin |
| shiny coat | brooding patch |
| orange beak | warm |
| white tummy | eggs |
| black eyes | hatch |
| orange hair | chicks |

## EMPHASIZE THESE HAVE-TO WORDS IN THIS THEME:

|  |  | |  | |
| --- | --- | --- | --- | --- |
| **that** | **go** | **on** | **live** | **went** |
| (stick out your tongue + "at") | (green light means "go") | (the dot is on the box) | (we live in a house) | (the car went down the street) |

## SENTENCE SQUARES SENTENCES

Penguins have black and white feathers.
They like to play.
Penguins have flippers to help them swim.
They slide on the ice.
Penguins like to swim in the water.

## SEQUENCE STORY PROMPT

Write a story that tells how a baby penguin chick is born.

# Picture Dictionary Words

**Directions:** Read each word. Cut out the picture cards and glue them in your Picture Dictionary.

| | | |
|---|---|---|
| 1. penguin | 2. ✚ black and white | 3. flippers |
| 4. web feet | 5. feathers | 6. ice |
| 7. water | 8. play | 9. swim |
| 10. slide | 11. fish | 12. r+ +k+er""E" rookery |

# Pocket Chart Words

**Descriptive Story** (Use with Let's Create It on page 72)

| | | |
|---|---|---|
| ✒ +"E"<br>**feathery** | 😷+👁+🦵 🧥<br>**shiny coat** | ☁ 😃←<br>**orange beak** |
| ☁ †+Ⓗ+🧍<br>**white tummy** | ☁ 👀<br>**black eyes** | ☁ 👩←<br>**orange hair** |

**Sequence Story** (Use with Sequence Story on page 77)

| | | |
|---|---|---|
| d+ă+"D"<br>**Daddy**<br>🐧<br>**Penguin** | br+👻+d+👑ing<br>**brooding**<br>▦<br>**patch** | W+🧍←<br>**warm** |
| ⬭⬭<br>**eggs** | 🥚<br>**hatch** | 🐤🐤<br>**chicks** |

Rebus Writing • Winter © 2004 Creative Teaching Press

# Word Hunt

**Directions:** Use your Picture Dictionary to help you find the word that goes with each picture. Write the correct word below each picture. Complete the special sentence at the bottom of the page.

  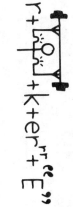

# Secret Sentence Booklet

**Directions:** Write the correct word under each rebus picture.

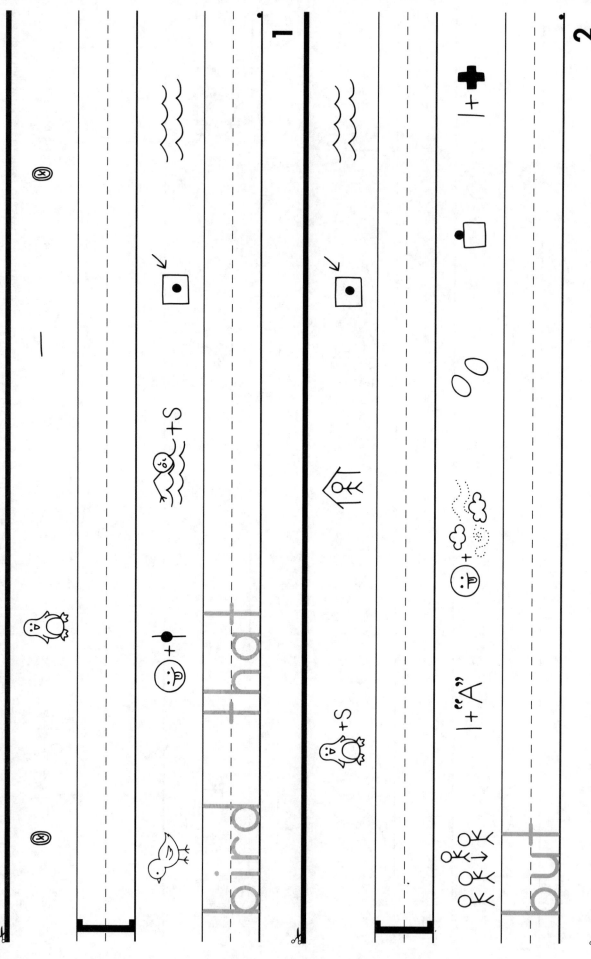

Rebus Writing • Winter © 2004 Creative Teaching Press

2

$+S^{ss}$

3

$+A$ "`·`"

hatch

$r+$ $+k+er^{rr}$ "`E`"

4

Rebus Writing • Winter © 2004 Creative Teaching Press

# Bubble Writing

**Directions:** Write the correct word in each bubble. Use these words to complete the sentences at the bottom of the page.

Rebus Writing • Winter © 2004 Creative Teaching Press

# Connect a Sentence

**Directions:** Read the phrase in the center bubble. Add words from the connecting bubbles to the phrase to make a sentence. Use additional words to create more sentences. Write the sentences on a separate piece of paper.

to find food

to live in the snow

to go to a rookery

to slide on ice

feathers to keep warm

to swim in cold water

Penguins have

black flippers

to grow new feathers

web feet

a white tummy

an orange beak

a shiny coat

black and white feathers

# Sentence Squares

**Directions:** Read the word cards. Cut apart the cards and mix them up. Make sure that the words are face up. Use the word cards to make sentences.

| Penguins | play | They | help |
|----------|------|------|------|
| have | them | are | ice | black |
| and | white | the | to | swim |
| web feet | | feathers | | in |
| on | flippers | slide | water | like |

Rebus Writing • Winter © 2004 Creative Teaching Press

# Sentence/Story Builder

**Directions:** Use the pictures to help you write a sentence or story that describes who, what, when, where, and why.

| When | Who | Is Doing What | Where | Why |
|---|---|---|---|---|
| one time | penguins | playing | zoo | keep cool |

# Story Box

**Directions:** Use the picture box ideas to write a story.

Character

Daddy Penguin

Setting

rookery

1

brooding patch and egg

2

chick hatching

3

Daddy Penguin goes to water

Rebus Writing • Winter © 2004 Creative Teaching Press

# Backward Story

**Directions:** Read the ending of the story and then tell what might have happened at the beginning and in the middle of the story.

### QUESTIONS FOR PROMPTING

- Where were the penguins?
- Why were they there?
- Why did the Daddy Penguin stay?
- What did he do?

_____

_____

_____

_____

_____

_____

_____

_____

_____

_____

**Then    the    Daddy    Penguin    went    to    the    water**

**to    get    fish.**

Rebus Writing • Winter © 2004 Creative Teaching Press

# Let's Create It

(Note to the teacher: Copy a class set of the Penguin Pattern reproducible on heavy tagboard or card stock to create patterns for the penguin's body, feet, and beak. Copy a class set of the Penguin Parts pattern on white construction paper.)

## MATERIALS

- ✓ tagboard or card stock
- ✓ white, black, and orange construction paper
- ✓ white chalk
- ✓ scissors
- ✓ glue
- ✓ crayons or markers
- ✓ Picture Dictionary
- ✓ Descriptive Story Pocket Chart Words reproducible (page 62)

**STEP 1**

Place the penguin patterns on a piece of black construction paper. Use chalk to trace the pattern onto the paper. Cut out the penguin body. Cut out the white tummy, flippers, and eyes and glue them onto the penguin body. Use a black crayon or marker to color the eyes. Place the feet and beak patterns on a piece of orange construction paper. Use a pencil to trace the patterns onto the paper. Cut out the feet and beak and glue them on the penguin body.

## Penguin Parts

**STEP 2**

Use your Picture Dictionary and the pocket chart words to help you write a sentence or story about your penguin on a separate piece of paper.

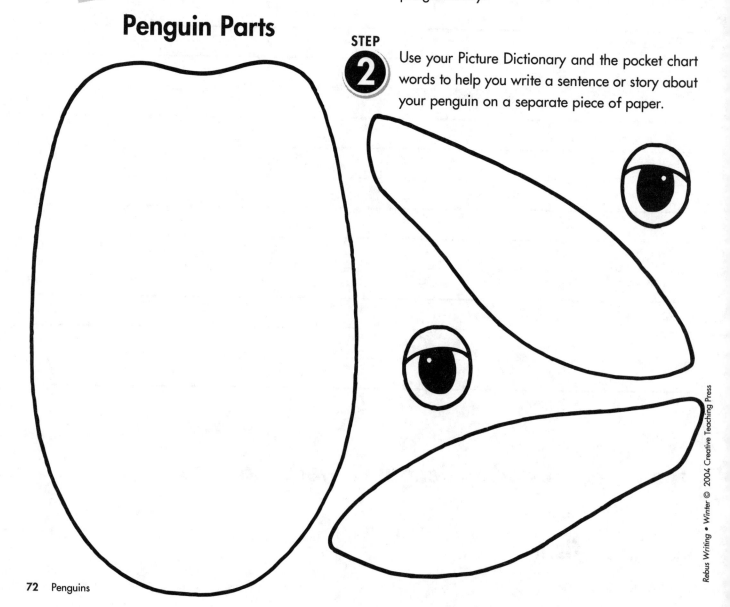

Rebus Writing • Winter © 2004 Creative Teaching Press

# Penguin Pattern

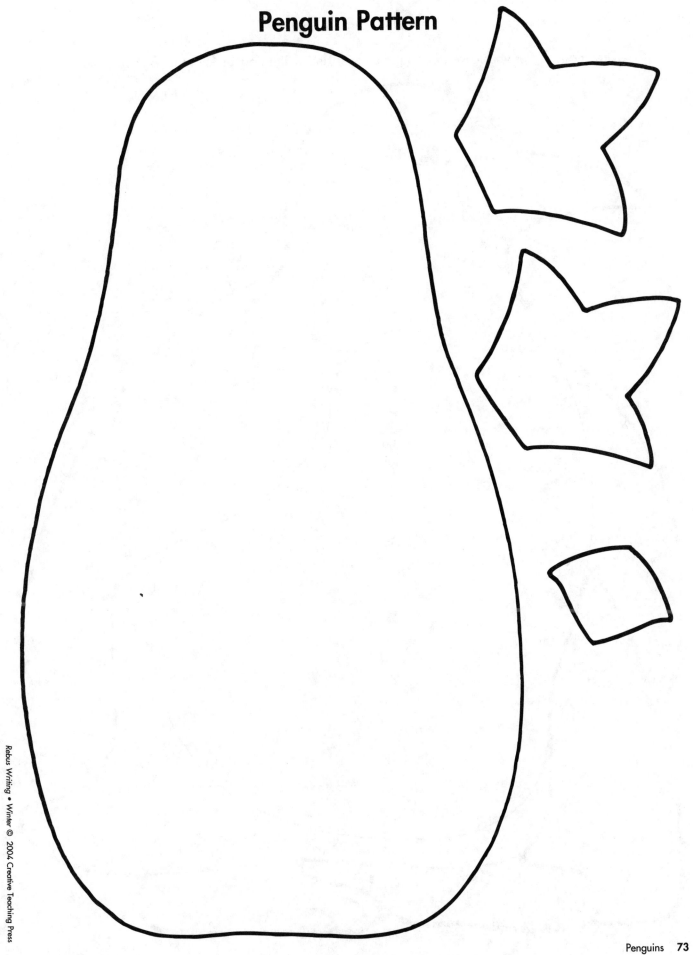

# Shape Book

**Directions:** Color your cover. Cut out the cover and writing paper to create a shape book.

# Word Web

**Directions:** Use the words on the word web to help you write a story.

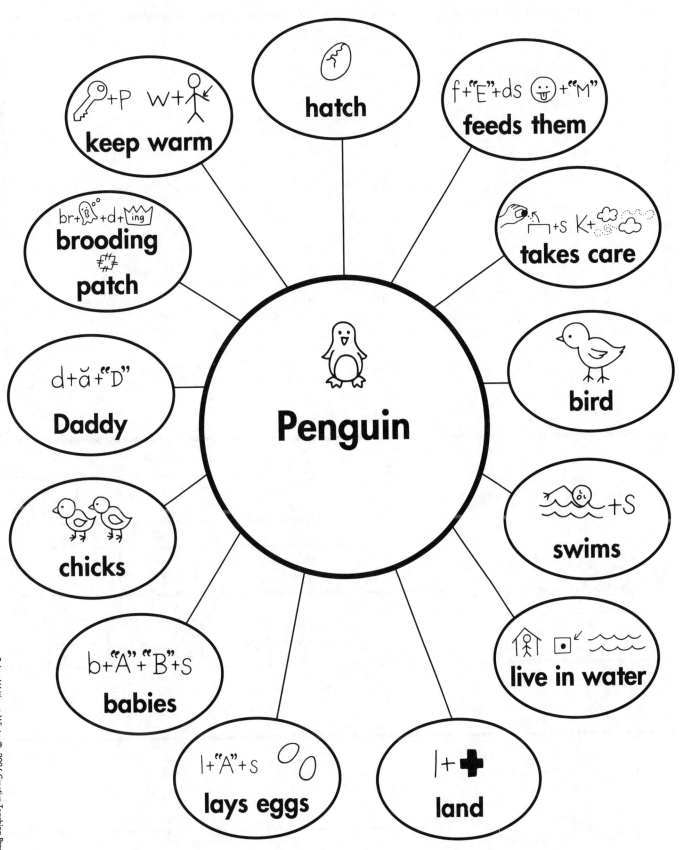

# Class Book

**Directions:** Use words from your Picture Dictionary and around the room to help you complete the sentences. Draw a picture to go with your sentences.

I saw a _____. He

was _____ and

_____. He liked to

_____.

By _____

Rebus Writing • Winter © 2004 Creative Teaching Press

Name_____

# Sequence Story

**Directions:** Color the pictures and cut them out. Glue the picture cards in order in the numbered boxes to show the sequence of the penguin laying an egg. Use the picture cards to write a story on another piece of paper. Use your Picture Dictionary and the Sequence Story Pocket Chart Words to help you.

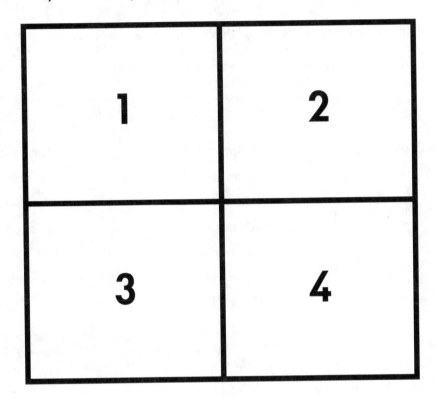

# Groundhogs  +S

The activities in this theme emphasize the use of describing words and sequence of events. Additional vocabulary is introduced to promote descriptive writing and seasons.

## READ-ALOUDS

**Fluffy Meets the Groundhog**
by Kate McMullan
(SCHOLASTIC)

**Gretchen Groundhog, It's Your Day!**
by Abby Levine
(ALBERT WHITMAN AND COMPANY)

**Groundhog Day**
by Don Yoder
(STACKPOLE BOOKS)

**How Groundhog's Garden Grew**
by Lynne Cherry
(BLUE SKY PRESS)

**The Secret of the First One Up**
by Iris Hiskey Arno
(NORTHWORD PRESS)

## PICTURE DICTIONARY WORDS

**groundhog
shy
claws
bushy tail
digs
underground
hides
peeks out
hole
burrow
shadow
spring**

## POCKET CHART WORDS

| **Descriptive Story** | **Sequence Story** |
|---|---|
| big front teeth | hibernates |
| short whiskers | winter |
| thick brown fur | grass and berries |
| small round eyes | danger |
| two front paws | whistles |
| chubby body | safe |

## EMPHASIZE THESE HAVE-TO WORDS IN THIS THEME:

| ↑ | ↓ | ⓜf | | |
|---|---|---|---|---|
| **up** | **down** | **of** | **his** | **all** |
| | | (the belly button sound + /f/) | (/h/ + is) | (ball without the "b") |

## SENTENCE SQUARES SENTENCES

The groundhog is hairy and brown.
It is cute, chubby, and shy.
It digs a hole underground.
The groundhog is scared of its shadow.

## SEQUENCE STORY PROMPT

Write a story about how groundhogs protect themselves.

# Picture Dictionary Words

**Directions:** Read each word. Cut out the picture cards and glue them in your Picture Dictionary.

| | | |
|---|---|---|
| 1. **groundhog** | 2. **shy** | 3. **claws** |
| 4. **bushy tail** | 5. **digs** | 6. **underground** |
| 7. **hides** | 8. **peeks out** | 9. **hole** |
| 10. **burrow** | 11. **shadow** | 12. **spring** |

# Pocket Chart Words

**Descriptive Story** (Use with Let's Create It on page 90)

| | | |
|---|---|---|
| **big** **front teeth** | **short** **whiskers** | **thick** **brown fur** |
| **small** **round eyes** | **two** **front paws** | **chubby body** |

**Sequence Story** (Use with Sequence Story on page 94)

| | | |
|---|---|---|
| **hibernates** | **winter** | **grass and** **berries** |
| **danger** | **whistles** | **safe** |

Rebus Writing • Winter © 2004 Creative Teaching Press

# Word Hunt

**Directions:** Use your Picture Dictionary to help you find the word that goes with each picture. Write the correct word below each picture. Complete the special sentence at the bottom of the page.

_____  _____  _____  _____

  SP+

_____  _____

b+er"o"

_____

b+ + s  + s

_____  _____  _____  _____

  b+er"o"

_____  ⊗  _____

**Directions:** Write the correct word under each rebus picture.

b+a

+s

1

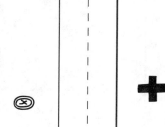

lives

2

Rebus Writing • Winter © 2004 Creative Teaching Press

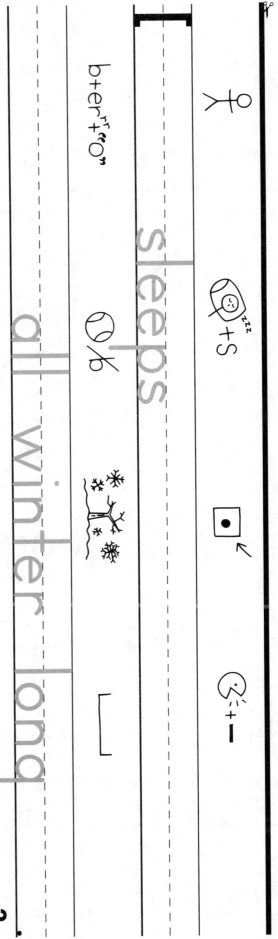

b+err"o"

sleeps    all winter long

if    ~f

4    S+"e"A"+f

3

# Bubble Writing

**Directions:** Write the correct word in each bubble. Use these words to complete the sentences at the bottom of the page.

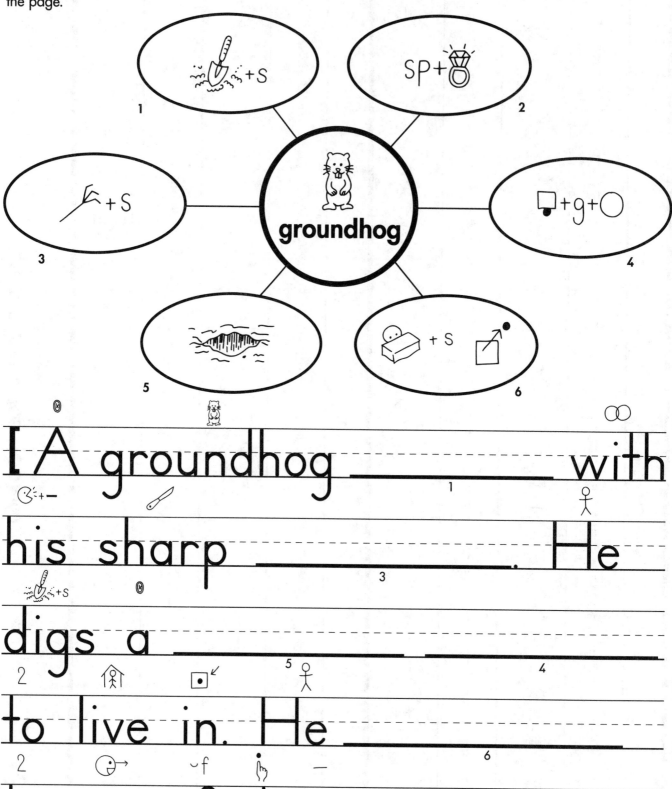

Rebus Writing • Winter © 2004 Creative Teaching Press

# Connect a Sentence

**Directions:** Read the phrase in the center bubble. Add words from the connecting bubbles to the phrase to make a sentence. Use additional words to create more sentences. Write the sentences on a separate piece of paper.

# Sentence Squares

**Directions:** Read the word cards. Cut apart the cards and mix them up. Make sure that the words are face up. Use the word cards to make sentences.

| | | | |
|---|---|---|---|
| The | and | groundhog | hairy |
| hole | digs | shadow | is · its |
| It | a | brown | . · in |
| shy | underground | chubby | peeks |
| out | of | cute | burrow · scared |

Rebus Writing • Winter © 2004 Creative Teaching Press

# Sentence/Story Builder

**Directions:** Use the pictures to help you write a sentence or story that describes who, what, when, where, and why.

| When | Who | Is Doing What | Where | Why |
|---|---|---|---|---|
| day | groundhog | climbs | outside | wake up |

Rebus Writing • Winter © 2004 Creative Teaching Press

# Story Box

**Directions:** Use the picture box ideas to write a story.

| Character | Setting |
|---|---|
| groundhog | hole |

| 1 | 2 | 3 |
|---|---|---|
| peeks out | shadow | sleep |

_____

- - - - - - - - - - - - - - - - - - - -

_____

- - - - - - - - - - - - - - - - - - - -

_____

- - - - - - - - - - - - - - - - - - - -

_____

- - - - - - - - - - - - - - - - - - - -

_____

Rebus Writing • Winter © 2004 Creative Teaching Press

# Backward Story

**Directions:** Read the ending of the story and then tell what might have happened at the beginning and in the middle of the story.

**QUESTIONS FOR PROMPTING**

- Why was the groundhog sleeping in his burrow? (hibernation)
- Why did the groundhog come out of his burrow?
- Was it sunny or cloudy?
- Why did the groundhog care if spring was coming or not?

_____

- - - - - - - - - - - - - - - - - - - - - -

_____

- - - - - - - - - - - - - - - - - - - - - -

_____

- - - - - - - - - - - - - - - - - - - - - -

_____

- - - - - - - - - - - - - - - - - - - - - -

_____

- - - - - - - - - - - - - - - - - - - - - -

_____

**Then    the    groundhog    ran    back    into    his    burrow.**

Rebus Writing • Winter © 2004 Creative Teaching Press

# Let's Create It

MATERIALS

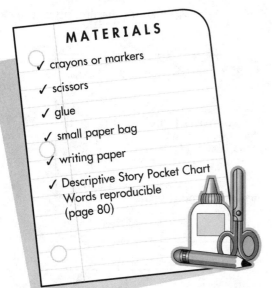

✓ crayons or markers

✓ scissors

✓ glue

✓ small paper bag

✓ writing paper

✓ Descriptive Story Pocket Chart Words reproducible (page 80)

**STEP 1** Color the groundhog puppet pieces. Cut out the pieces and glue them to the bottom of a folded paper bag to create a puppet.

**STEP 2** Use your Picture Dictionary and the pocket chart words to help you write a story about the groundhog on a separate piece of paper.

## Groundhog Puppet

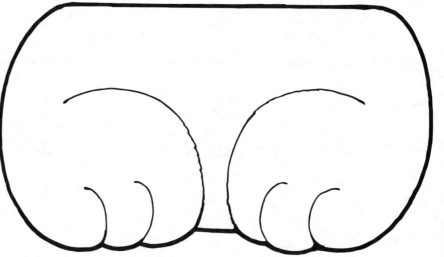

# Shape Book

**Directions:** Color your cover. Cut out the cover and writing paper to create a shape book.

# Word Web

**Directions:** Use the words on the word web to help you write a story.

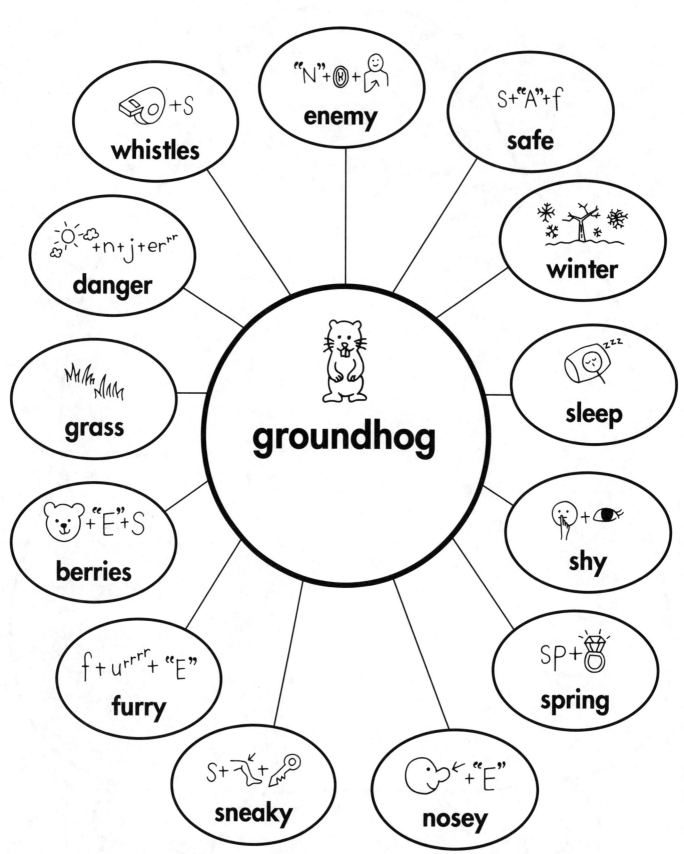

# Class Book

**Directions:** Use words from your Picture Dictionary and around the room to help you complete the sentences. Draw a picture to go with your sentences.

Once upon a time, I saw

a _____. He looked

_____ and _____.

He had _____ and

_____. He liked to

_____.

By _____

# Sequence Story

**Directions:** Color the pictures and cut them out. Glue the picture cards in order in the numbered boxes to show the sequence of the groundhog's day. Use the picture cards to write a story on another piece of paper. Use your Picture Dictionary and the Sequence Story Pocket Chart Words to help you.

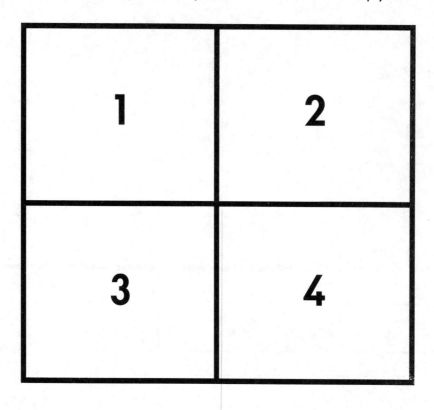

# Friends

 + S

Use this theme in conjunction with Valentine's Day to teach children about friendship. The activities in this theme emphasize the qualities of friendship. Additional vocabulary is introduced to promote descriptive and seasonal writing related to Valentine's Day.

## READ-ALOUDS

***Best Friends***
by Steven Kellogg
(DUTTON)

***Best Friends for Frances***
by Russell Hoban
(HARPERTROPHY)

***Friends***
by Helme Heine
(ALADDIN)

***May I Bring A Friend?***
by Beatrice Schenk de Regniers
(ATHENEUM BOOKS)

***A Rainbow of Friends***
by P.K. Hallinan
(IDEALS CHILDREN'S BOOKS)

## PICTURE DICTIONARY WORDS

**friend
fair
helpful
cheerful
nice
play
work
share
care
together
each other
take turns**

## POCKET CHART WORDS

| Descriptive Story | Sequence Story |
|---|---|
| kind | special |
| thoughtful | do nice things |
| polite | friendly |
| caring | nice to people |
| considerate | make me happy |
| giving | play with me |

## EMPHASIZE THESE HAVE-TO WORDS IN THIS THEME:

**we**

(girl + boy = we)

"u"

**you**

**us**

(pointing to each other—us)

**give**

(give me the dot)

"B"+K+Zᶻᶻ

**because**

("B" + /k/ + /z/)

## SENTENCE SQUARES SENTENCES

Friends are nice to each other.
They work and play together.
My friends are fair and take turns.
They like to play with each other.
Friends are helpful and work together.

## SEQUENCE STORY PROMPT

Write a story about making and sending a valentine to someone special.

# Picture Dictionary Words

**Directions:** Read each word. Cut out the picture cards and glue them in your Picture Dictionary.

| | | |
|---|---|---|
| **1.** | **2.** | **3.** |
| **friend** | **fair** | **helpful** |
| **4.** | **5.** | **6.** |
| **cheerful** | **nice** | **play** |
| **7.** | **8.** | **9.** |
| **work** | **share** | **care** |
| **10.** | **11.** | **12.** |
| **together** | **each other** | **take turns** |

Rebus Writing • Winter © 2004 Creative Teaching Press

# Pocket Chart Words

## Descriptive Story (Use with Let's Create It on page 107)

| K+👁+nd | ☺ᵒ + 🥤 | 🚩+💡 |
|---|---|---|
| **kind** | **thoughtful** | **polite** |
| K+☁+👑(ing) | k+n+Sˢˢ+d+er+👆 | 🧑🎈🧑+👑(ing) |
| **caring** | **considerate** | **giving** |

## Sequence Story (Use with Sequence Story on page 111)

| SP+😶+l | d+👻ᵒᵒ  n+🧊 <br> **do nice** <br> 😛+👑(ing)+S | 🤝+l+"E" |
|---|---|---|
| **special** | **things** | **friendly** |
| n+🧊  2 <br> **nice to** <br> 🧍🧍🧍🧍 | m+"A"+K  m+"E" <br> **make me** <br> ☺ | 🏏🧍  ⊂⊃ <br> **play with** <br> m+"E" |
| **people** | **happy** | **me** |

# Word Hunt

**Directions:** Use your Picture Dictionary to help you find the word that goes with each picture. Write the correct word below each picture. Complete the special sentence at the bottom of the page.

  K +  n +

_ _ _ _ _ _ _ _ _ _ _ _ _ _ _ _ _ _ _ _ _ _ _ _ _

+ 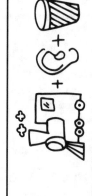 +  +  2 + + er$^{rr}$

_ _ _ _ _ _ _ _ _ _ _ _ _ _ _ _ _ _ _ _ _ _ _ _ _

" E " + 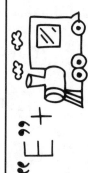 + er$^{rr}$  + S

_ _ _ _ _ _ _ _ _ _ _ _ _ _ _ _ _ _ _ _ _ _ _ _ _

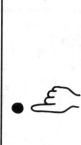 — n + 2 + S

_ _ _ _ _ _ _ _ _ _ _ _ _ _ _ _ _ _ _ _ _ _ _ _ _

*Rebus Writing • Winter* © 2004 Creative Teaching Press

# Secret Sentence Booklet

**Directions:** Write the correct word under each rebus picture.

m+

+S

"R"

n+

---

m+"E"

m+"A"+K

m+"E"

make

---

+"A"

m+"E"

+

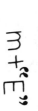

m+"E"

with

# Secret Sentence Booklet

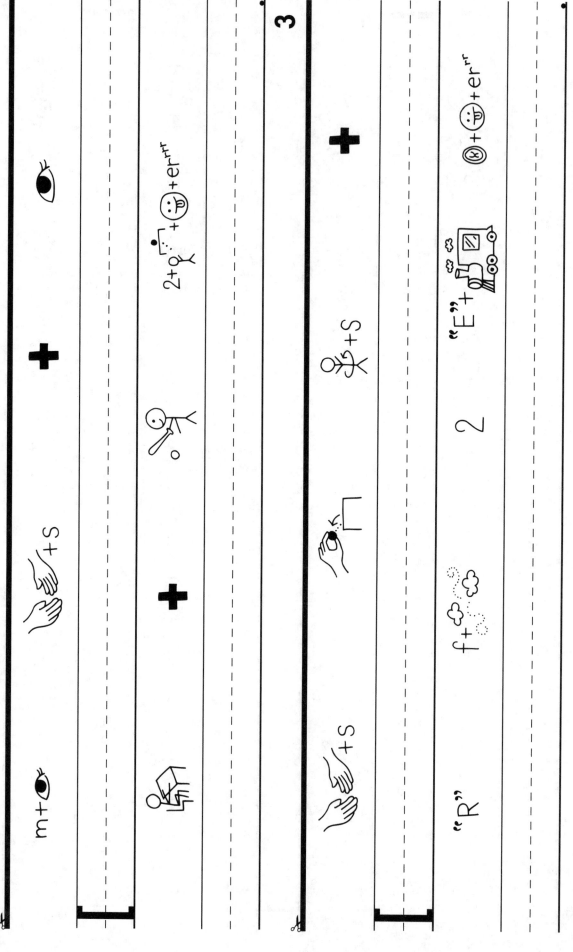

Rebus Writing • Winter © 2004 Creative Teaching Press

# Bubble Writing

**Directions:** Write the correct word in each bubble. Use these words to complete the sentences at the bottom of the page.

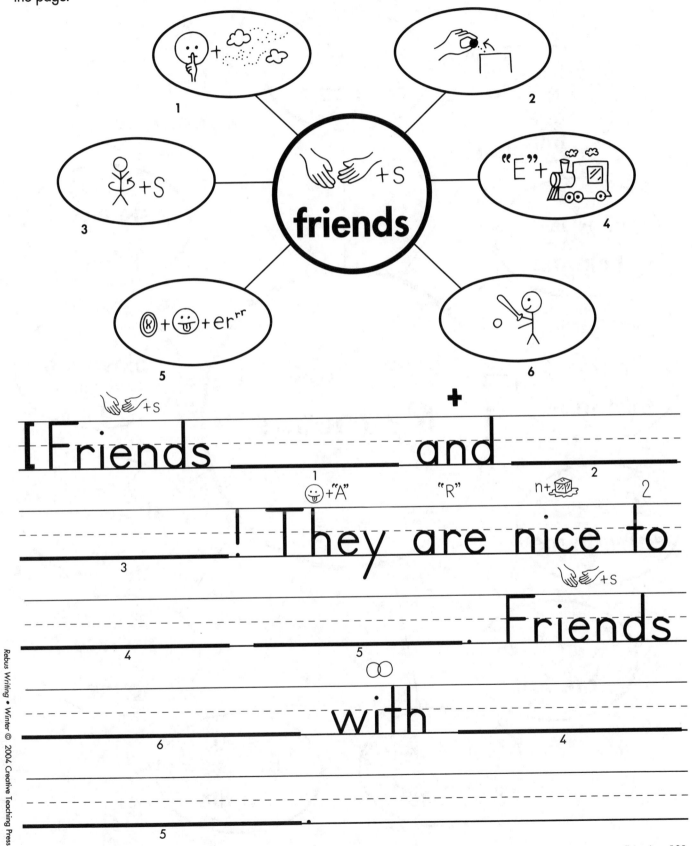

# Connect a Sentence

**Directions:** Read the phrase in the center bubble. Add words from the connecting bubbles to the phrase to make a sentence. Use additional words to create more sentences. Write the sentences on a separate piece of paper.

Rebus Writing • Winter © 2004 Creative Teaching Press

# Sentence Squares

**Directions:** Read the word cards. Cut apart the cards and mix them up. Make sure that the words are face up. Use the word cards to make sentences.

| | | | | |
|---|---|---|---|---|
| Friends | play | They | work | are |
| like | with | to | happy | nice |
| helpful | and | each | other | fair |
| cheerful | take | turns | My | |
| together | . | | | |

# Sentence/Story Builder

**Directions:** Use the pictures to help you write a sentence or story that describes who, what, when, where, and why.

| When | Who | Is Doing What | Where | Why |
|---|---|---|---|---|
| Valentine's Day | friends | making valentines | school | happy |

Rebus Writing • Winter © 2004 Creative Teaching Press

# Story Box

**Directions:** Use the picture box ideas to write a story.

## Characters

friends

## Setting

PLANETS

classroom

### 1
making valentines

### 2
delivering valentines

### 3
glowing faces

# Backward Story

**Directions:** Read the ending of the story and then tell what might have happened at the beginning and in the middle of the story.

## QUESTIONS FOR PROMPTING

- What special day was it?
- Where did the valentines come from?
- How were the valentines delivered?
- When were they opened?

_____

- - - - - - - - - - - - - - - - - - - - - -

_____

- - - - - - - - - - - - - - - - - - - - - -

_____

- - - - - - - - - - - - - - - - - - - - - -

_____

- - - - - - - - - - - - - - - - - - - - - -

_____

**When    I    got    home,    I    showed    my    mom    all**

**the    valentines    I    got    at    school.**

Rebus Writing • Winter © 2004 Creative Teaching Press

# Let's Create It

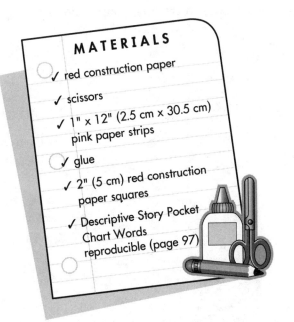

## MATERIALS

- ✓ red construction paper
- ✓ scissors
- ✓ 1" x 12" (2.5 cm x 30.5 cm) pink paper strips
- ✓ glue
- ✓ 2" (5 cm) red construction paper squares
- ✓ Descriptive Story Pocket Chart Words reproducible (page 97)

(Note to the teacher: Copy the pattern below onto a piece of red construction paper for each child.)

**STEP 1**

Cut out the valentine pattern. Fold it in half width-wise so the lines are showing. Start on the straight edge and cut only on the lines. Take three pink paper strips and place them through the slits to make a weave. Glue them to the backside of the top part of the heart. Cut out three hearts from the red paper squares and glue them to the bottom of the pink paper strips.

**STEP 2**

Write **Friends Are** on the top part of your large heart and write three words on the bottom hearts that describe your friends.

# Shape Book

**Directions:** Color your cover. Cut out the cover and writing paper to create a shape book.

Rebus Writing • Winter © 2004 Creative Teaching Press

# Word Web

**Directions:** Use the words on the word web to help you write a story.

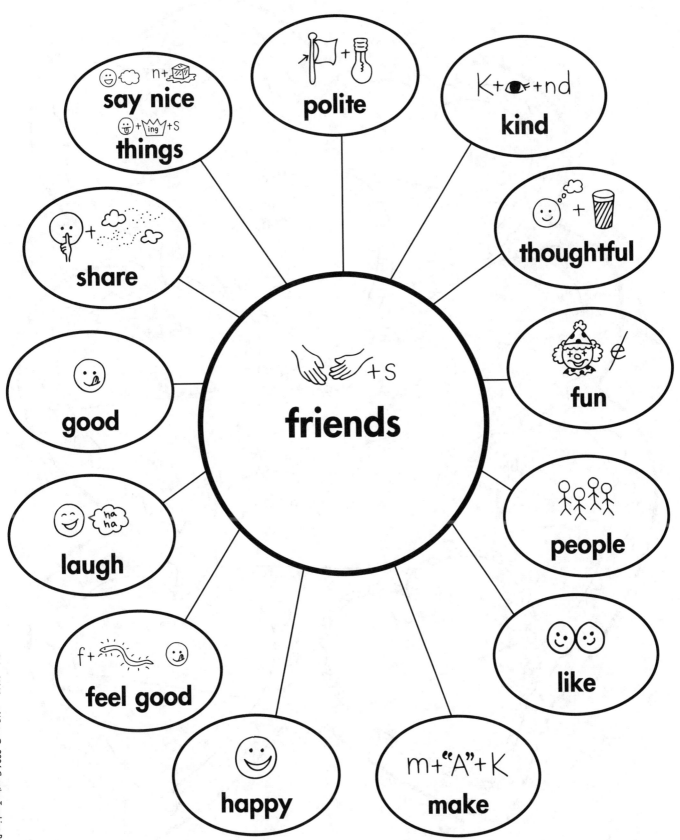

# Class Book

**Directions:** Interview a friend about his or her favorite things. Write your friend's answers in the hearts. Color each heart.

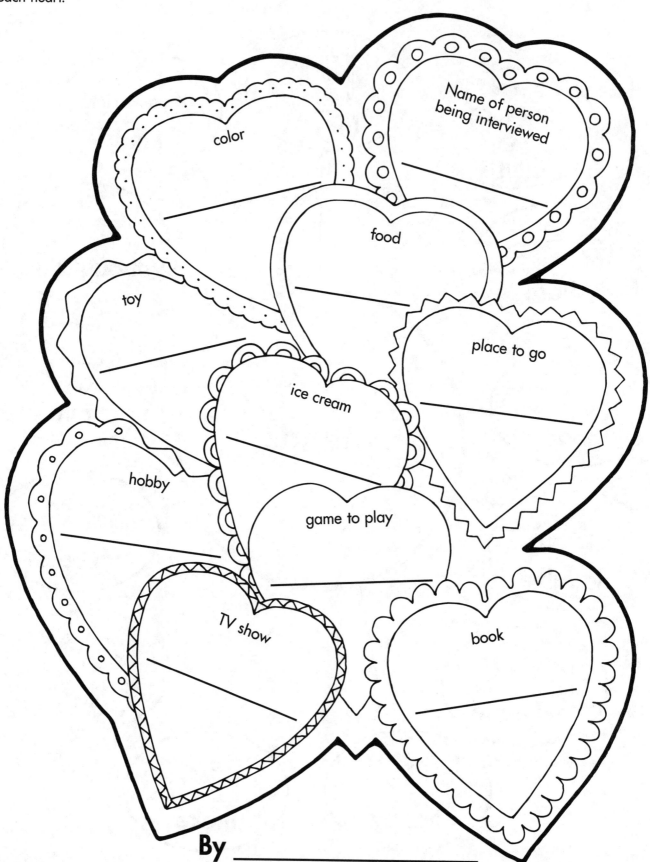

color

Name of person being interviewed

food

toy

place to go

ice cream

hobby

game to play

TV show

book

By _____

Rebus Writing • Winter © 2004 Creative Teaching Press

# Sequence Story

**Directions:** Color the pictures and cut them out. Glue the picture cards in order in the numbered boxes to show the sequence of a child making a valentine card. Use the picture cards to write a story on another piece of paper. Use your Picture Dictionary and the Sequence Story Pocket Chart Words to help you.

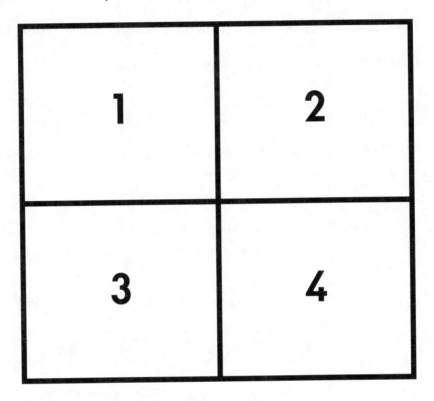

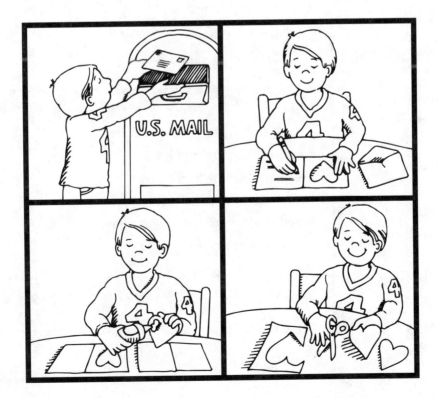

# Presidents

The activities in this theme emphasize informational writing. Additional vocabulary is introduced to promote descriptive writing, seasonal writing related to Presidents' Day, and drawing conclusions.

## READ-ALOUDS

***George Washington and the General's Dog***
by Richard Walz
(RANDOM HOUSE)

***Hail to the Chief: The American Presidency***
by Don Robb
(CHARLESBRIDGE PUBLISHING)

***A Picture Book of Abraham Lincoln***
by David A. Adler
(HOLIDAY HOUSE)

***Presidents' Day***
by David F. Marx
(CHILDREN'S PRESS)

***So You Want to Be President?***
by Judith St. George
(PHILOMEL)

## PICTURE DICTIONARY WORDS

**presidents**
**brave**
**fair**
**honest**
**wise**
**leader**
**country**
**laws**
**people**
**rights**
**safe**
**freedom**

## POCKET CHART WORDS

| **Descriptive Story** | **Sequence Story** |
|---|---|
| top hat | campaign |
| log cabin | election |
| 16th president | vote |
| white wig | ceremony |
| army | inauguration |
| first president | White House |

## EMPHASIZE THESE HAVE-TO WORDS IN THIS THEME:

   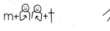

**our**
(/ou/ what we say when we hit our finger with a hammer + /r/)

**who**
(the sound an owl makes)

**if**

**must**
(/m/ + us + /t/)

**put**
(put the dot on the table)

## SENTENCE SQUARES SENTENCES

Presidents are fair and honest.
They must be wise and brave.
They make laws to help people.
Presidents have to lead the country.
They are wise leaders.

## SEQUENCE STORY PROMPT

Write a story telling about how someone becomes president.

# Picture Dictionary Words

**Directions:** Read each word. Cut out the picture cards and glue them in your Picture Dictionary.

| | | |
|---|---|---|
| 1. pr+s$^{ss}$+⊗+car<br><br>**president** | 2. br+☺<br><br>**brave** | 3. f+☁☁<br><br>**fair** |
| 4. ▢•+🐛<br><br>**honest** | 5. "Y"+Z$^{zz}$<br><br>**wise** | 6. ↓ ☺☺☺<br><br>**leader** |
| 7. K+⊗+n+🌲<br><br>**country** | 8. 👃$^P$+s<br><br>**laws** | 9. ☺☺☺☺<br><br>**people** |
| 10. r+👁+t+s<br><br>**rights** | 11. S+"A"+f<br><br>**safe** | 12. ✗+d+m<br><br>**freedom** |

# Pocket Chart Words

**Descriptive Story** (Use with Let's Create It on page 124)

| | | |
|---|---|---|
| log cabin | top hat | white wig |
| $16^{th}$ <br> **16**$^{th}$ <br> pr+s$^{ss}$+⊛+↓car <br> **president** | "R"+🙂 <br> **army** | $1^{st}$ <br> **first** <br> pr+s$^{ss}$+⊛+↓car <br> **president** |

**Sequence Story** (Use with Sequence Story on page 128)

| | | |
|---|---|---|
| k+m+p+"A"+n <br> **campaign** | "E"+l+k+🙂+n <br> **election** | v+"O"+† <br> **vote** |
| S+☁+⊚+m+"O"+🦵 <br> **ceremony** | "E"+n+g+er$^{rr}$+8+🙂+n <br> **inauguration** | 🏠 <br> **White House** |

Name _____

# Word Hunt

**Directions:** Use your Picture Dictionary to help you find the word that goes with each picture. Write the correct word below each picture. Complete the special sentence at the bottom of the page.

pr+S+ⓍⓄ +

br+ 😀

f+ ☁

🔲+ 🌟

"Y'" +Z^zz

✖+d+m

👥👥👥

K+ⓍⓄ+n+🌲

r+👁+t+s

S+"A"+f

_____

pr+S+ⓍⓄ +         🐦        K+ⓍⓄ+n+🌲

**runs**

# Secret Sentence Booklet

**Directions:** Write the correct word under each rebus picture.

pr+S<sup>ss</sup>+⊗+🚗    —    ⊗f    →😊😊😊🚶🚶🚶

👆

⊗    👉-👟+r    K+⊗+n+🌲

our

**1**

pr+S<sup>ss</sup>+⊗+🚗    ⊗    🐷🪑    K+⊗+n+🌲

👉-👟+r    🙈😾+S    2+🔑+😛+er<sup>rr</sup>

our

**2**

# Secret Sentence Booklet

pr+S$^{ss}$++    "R"    "Y"+Z$^{zz}$    ✚

+    ✚    K+    +b+    

m+"A"+K    +S    about

+"A"    +r    K++n+

our

3

4

Name_____

# Bubble Writing

**Directions:** Write the correct word in each bubble. Use these words to complete the sentences at the bottom of the page.

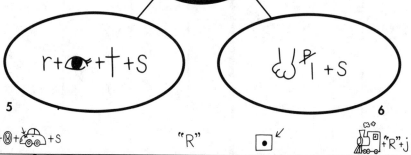

I Presidents are in charge of

_____ .

They make _____ to

_____ our _____

+ and keep _____ safe.

Rebus Writing • Winter © 2004 Creative Teaching Press

# Connect a Sentence

**Directions:** Read the phrase in the center bubble. Add words from the connecting bubbles to the phrase to make a sentence. Use additional words to create more sentences. Write the sentences on a separate piece of paper.

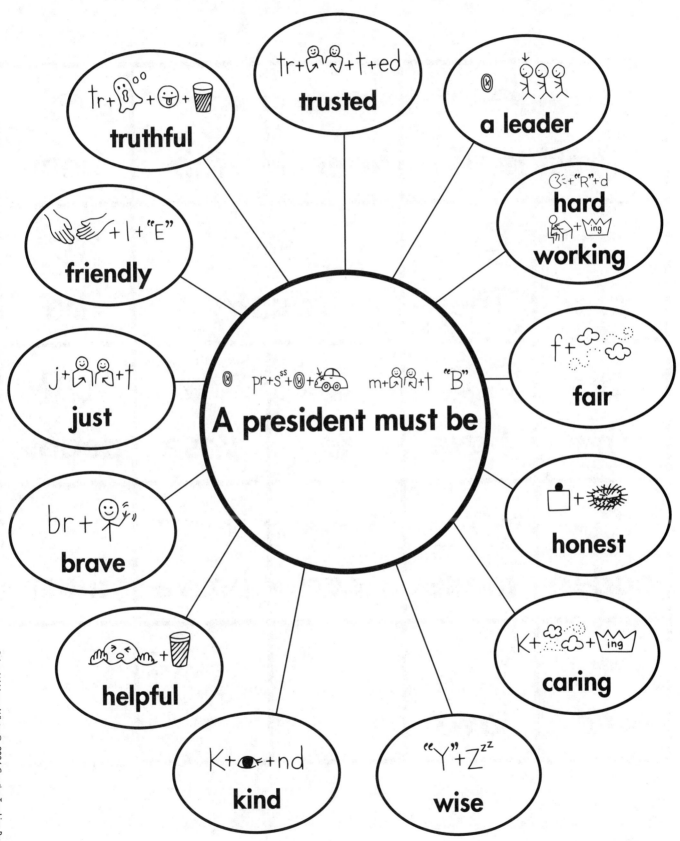

# Sentence Squares

**Directions:** Read the word cards. Cut apart the cards and mix them up. Make sure that the words are face up. Use the word cards to make sentences.

| pr+S^{ss}+⊛+🚗+s | ▢+🥚 | f+☁☁ | 🙌😫🙌 |
|---|---|---|---|
| **Presidents** | **honest** | **fair** | **help** |
| "R" | 😛+"A" | K+⊛+n+🌲 | "B" |
| **are** | **They** | **country** | **be** |
| 👉 | ✋ | 2 | "Y"+Z^{zz} | 🧍🧍🧍 |
| **the** | **have** | **to** | **wise** | **people** |
| 🧍🧍🧍+s | m+"A"+K | 🧍🧍🧍er | br+😃 | m+🧍🧍+t |
| **leaders** | **make** | **lead** | **brave** | **must** |
| ✚ | 👃+s | | | |
| **and** | **laws** | **.** | | |

Rebus Writing • Winter © 2004 Creative Teaching Press

# Sentence/Story Builder

**Directions:** Use the pictures to help you write a sentence or story that describes who, what, when, where, and why.

| When | Who | Is Doing What | Where | Why |
|---|---|---|---|---|
| a long time ago | Abe Lincoln | chopping wood | forest | log cabin |

# Story Box

**Directions:** Use the picture box ideas to write a story.

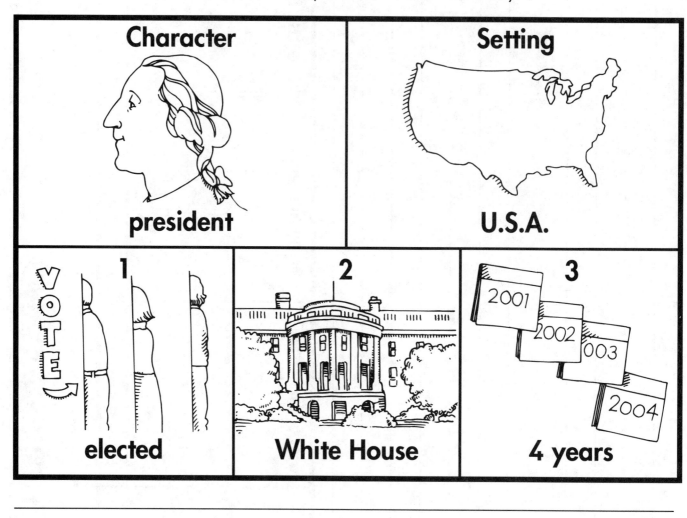

Character

president

Setting

U.S.A.

1 elected

2 White House

3 4 years

Rebus Writing • Winter © 2004 Creative Teaching Press

# Backward Story

**Directions:** Read the ending of the story and then tell what might have happened at the beginning and in the middle of the story.

| QUESTIONS FOR PROMPTING |
| --- |

- How do you become a president?
- What do you do as president?

_____

- - - - - - - - - - - - - - - - - - - - -

_____

- - - - - - - - - - - - - - - - - - - - -

_____

- - - - - - - - - - - - - - - - - - - - -

_____

- - - - - - - - - - - - - - - - - - - - -

_____

- - - - - - - - - - - - - - - - - - - - -

**That    is    why    a    president    is    so    important.**

# Let's Create It

**MATERIALS**
- ✓ scissors
- ✓ glue
- ✓ construction paper
- ✓ crayons or markers
- ✓ writing paper
- ✓ Descriptive Story Pocket Chart Words reproducible (page 114)

**STEP 1**
Cut apart the puzzle pieces and glue them together on a piece of construction paper to create two puzzles. Then color the puzzles.

**STEP 2**
Use your pocket chart words and Picture Dictionary to help you write a sentence or story about the presidents.

Rebus Writing • Winter © 2004 Creative Teaching Press

# Shape Book

**Directions:** Color your cover. Cut out the cover and writing paper to create a shape book.

# Word Web

**Directions:** Use the words on the word web to help you write a story.

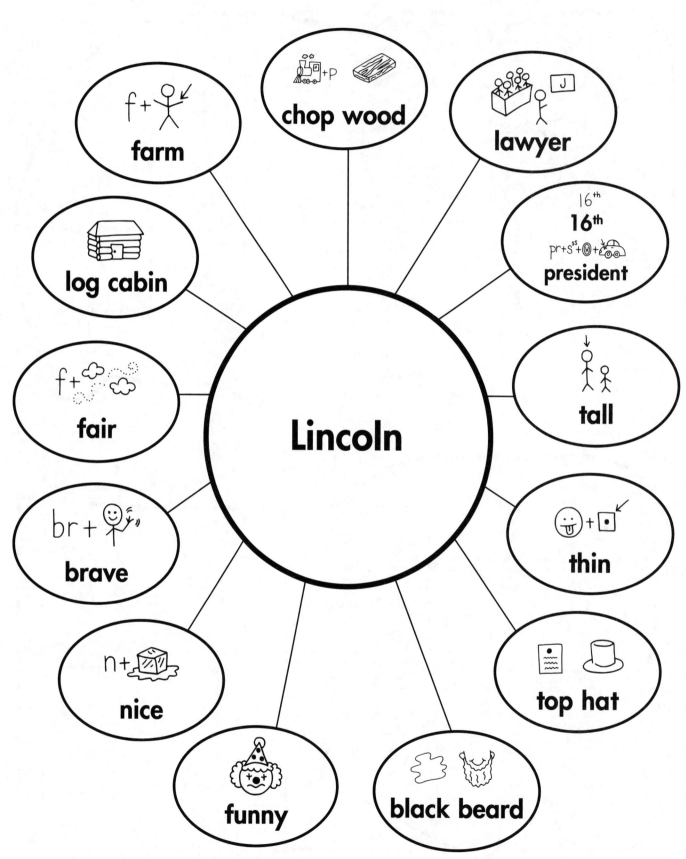

farm

chop wood

lawyer

16th president

log cabin

tall

fair

thin

brave

top hat

nice

funny

black beard

Lincoln

# Class Book

**Directions:** Use words from your Picture Dictionary and around the room to help you complete the sentences. Draw a picture to go with your sentences.

There once was a man

n+"A"+m+ed

named _____. He

was _____ and _____.

He had _____ and

_____. He was important

"B"+K+Z$^{zz}$

because _____.

By _____

# Sequence Story

**Directions:** Color the pictures and cut them out. Glue the picture cards in order in the numbered boxes to show the sequence of how a person becomes a president. Use the picture cards to write a story on another piece of paper. Use your Picture Dictionary and the Sequence Story Pocket Chart Words to help you.

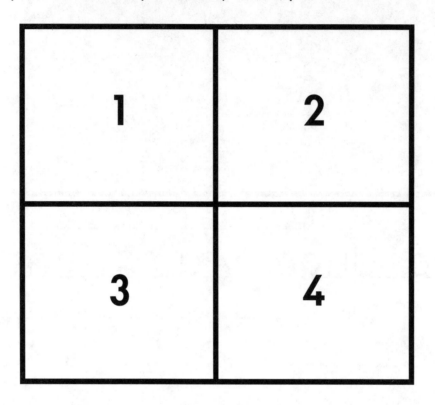